EMBRACING THE WORLD AS JESUS DID

by Jeff Kinley

Published by Cook Ministry Resources
a division of Cook Communications Ministries

4050 Lee Vance View
Colorado Springs, Colorado 80918

Colorado Springs, CO/Paris, Ontario
www.cookministries.com
Printed in U.S.A.

Author: Jeff Kinley
Designer: Rebekah Lyon
Editorial Team: Cheryl Crews, Frieda Nossaman, Jen Minnery

TABLE OF CONTENTS

Session 1: Live and in Person

Jesus Identified with the World   9

Session 2: Total Acceptance . . . No Exceptions

Jesus Showed Love to Sinners   21

Session 3: Jesus Experienced Things You Do

Jesus Demonstrated Compassion   33

Session 4: The Embrace of Love

Jesus Sacrificed Himself for Us   45

Session 5: **REALITY CHECK: PRACTICING YOUR EMBRACE**

Jesus Can Help Us Reach Out to Others   57

WHY DISCIPLESHIP?

Discipleship is a well-worn word. It's been used to justify everything from programs to events. But have you ever wondered what was in the mind of God when He invented the whole concept? His infinite wisdom could have created any method to accomplish His purpose in our lives. But this all-wise God simply told us to "make disciples."

Though there are many definitions for it, we could all agree that discipleship includes the process of learning and following Christ. And the bottom line is to become like Jesus, right? As Christians, we talk a lot about doing and not enough about being (God made us human beings, not human "doings"). He desires us to be conformed to the image of His Son (Romans 8:29). That process begins at salvation and continues until we arrive on heaven's shore.

So why disciple teenagers? Why not another program or "instant growth" gimmick? Why not entertainment or the newest ministry fad? Why discipleship?

First, because students need it. Pick up your newspaper or take a walk through the halls of your local high school if you need motivation. Second, Jesus commanded and modeled it. And third, history confirms it. Put simply, it works. It avoids the prevalent quick-fix, "decision" mentality and focuses instead on a long-term lifestyle. Discipleship is not a program. It's God's plan. It involves sharing with your students both the Word and your life, which leaves a lasting impact (1 Thessalonians 2:7-8).

Discipling teenagers doesn't require that they be good-looking, intelligent, well-balanced, or popular (think of the original dozen in Jesus' group!). It only requires students who are faithful learners and willing followers of Christ.

Some might say teenagers aren't ready for discipleship, that they can't handle the meat of the Word or the challenge of following Christ. Theirs is sort of a "junior Christianity." They don't have what it takes to become great for God. But we know better, don't we? So did Joseph, David, Daniel, Shadrach, Meshach, Abednego, Mary, and John Mark.

So does God.

The original Twelve disciples weren't much when they began, but they changed the course of human history. If we only had the first part of their story, we wouldn't hold out much hope for them—knowing their frequent faults and failures. But you know the rest of the story. The same is true for your students. The rest of their story is yet to be written. That's where you come in. This book is actually divided into two parts: Part One is contained in the following pages. But Part Two is yet to be written—and God has given you the opportunity to be part of writing that story as you touch your students' hearts with your life day by day.

This world desperately needs Christian youth to rise up and to answer the call of Christ to "come follow Me." This book will help them do that.

So pour your life into them. Impart the Word to them. Believe in them. Don't give up on them. Disciple them. And most of all,

Enjoy the journey!
Jeff Kinley

WHY CUSTOM DISCIPLESHIP?

So, you're convinced that what your students need is discipleship. So, why *Custom Discipleship*? Because *Custom Discipleship* acknowledges and deals with the two seemingly contradictory but central truths of discipleship.

1. There are Biblical principles that remain constant for all disciples of Jesus.
Custom Discipleship teaches students about the life of Christ and the example He set for Christians. Those stories are unchanging. The truths that Jesus communicated through word and example are the principles by which all Christians can truly live.

2. Discipleship is a dynamic, ever-changing process.
Custom Discipleship provides options that allow you to customize the learning process to meet the needs of the students in your group—no matter where they are in their relationship with Christ. This ability to customize the material keeps it dynamic and relevant to the lives of your students. Each lesson also contains *Learner Links* and *Making it Real* discipleship tips to help small-group leaders learn to share their lives with students and to grow alongside the students they are leading.

Custom Discipleship is a curriculum designed to blend the power of these truths. Let it help you as you take the challenge to disciple youth and obey Christ's command to make disciples.

Jeff Kinley is a veteran student minister, dedicated to students, parents, and youth workers as a life calling. He is the author of several successful books, including No Turning Back, Never the Same *and* Done Deal, *(David C. Cook Church Resources). A gifted communicator, Jeff is a frequent speaker at conferences and youth camps. Jeff and his wife Beverly, have three sons—Clayton, Stuart and Davis.*

KEY QUESTIONS are the focus of the lesson. Students should be able to answer these by the end of the session.

BIBLE BASE gives the scripture references that are the basis for the whole session.

THE OPENER is optional to the session. It is a great way to get kids involved before diving into the study.

SUPPLIES listed here are those needed for the core lesson. Any supplies for options are listed with that optional activity.

BOLD TYPE signifies "teacher talk"—things to be said directly by the leader of the group.

SESSION 3

WHAT A SERVANT FEELS

Key Questions
- How do our own painful experiences equip us to help others who are hurting?
- What kind of an example did Jesus set when it came to empathizing with people who are hurting?
- How can you empathize with hurting people?

Bible Base
Matthew 25:31-46
John 11:1-44
Romans 12:15

Supplies
- Flip chart
- Pens
- Pencils or pens
- Index cards
- Copies of Resources 3A, 3B, and Journal

Opener (Optional)

Common Ground
Ask your students to pull their chairs into a circle. Choose one of your group members to start the game standing in the middle of the circle. Remove his or her chair from the circle (think Musical Chairs). The person in the middle will call out a category. The category may be anything from "Collects comic books" to "Born in another state" to "Hates country music." Everyone in the group who fits the category must stand up and run to an empty seat. The person in the middle, meanwhile, must also try to get to an open chair. The person who doesn't make it must then stand in the middle and call out the next category.

MAKING IT REAL
As you get to know your students better, pray for them specifically. Taking the time to do this will help you to focus on their needs. It will also help you to continually acknowledge and trust that it is God who is making these kids into disciples of Jesus Christ—sometimes even in spite of your efforts!

This activity may prove to be an effective bonding exercise for your group members. They may be surprised to find out that other people in the group share their interests, experiences, or background.

CUSTOM DISCIPLESHIP 33

THERE ARE THREE LINKS that divide each session, taking students through the learning process and into personal application.

LEARNER LINKS are located through the sessions to give the leader extra tips on how to help their students learn the Word of God.

MAKING IT REAL sections are tips on discipleship located throughout the sessions.

OPTION ICONS are located at the beginning of each link to let you know that there are options for those groups at the end of the session.

RESOURCE PAGES are noted throughout the session. The actual pages are reproducible and can be found at the end of each session.

---

reasons God allows us to experience pain, suffering, loss, and hard times is so that we will be better able to understand what other hurting people are going through and be better prepared to help them? Why or why not? Let your group members offer their opinions.

Link 3
Empathy 'n' Me
Ask: Have you ever had someone say to you, "I know just how you're feeling"? If so, how did you feel when you heard those words? Did you believe the person? Why or why not? These words are especially popular at funerals. Usually the people who use the phrase don't mean any disrespect by it; they just might not know what else to say.

What if the person really did know how you feel—somewhat, at least? What if he or she had gone through a similar experience? Would you be interested in talking to that person? Why?

After a few students have offered their thoughts, say: Okay, let's reverse the situation. Let's say you run into someone who's hurting or in need of help. Let's say that the person is going through a situation similar to one you went through a year or so ago. Would you be interested in talking to that person? If some of your group members express reluctance, listen to their reasons for not getting involved. Invite the rest of the group to respond to those reasons.

The resource sheet "What I've Got to Give" (Resource 3B) is designed to help your group members identify the things in their lives that qualify them to be truly empathetic, the situations and circumstances they've experienced that make them experts of sorts in dealing with specific kinds of hurt. Encourage your students to take this assignment seriously. Emphasize that no one will be asked to share anything on the sheet that he or she is uncomfortable with.

LEARNER LINK
If any of your group members are brave enough to share their responses to Resource 3B, you will need to respect their feelings, as well as their privacy. You may need to ask a few questions to clarify a point or to correct a possible misunderstanding, but try not to pry for more information. Do not put your students in a position where they feel pressure to reveal more than they want to. When your volunteers finish sharing, be quick to affirm them, and encourage the rest of the group to do the same.

MAKING IT REAL
A big part of discipleship is encouraging your students to put into what they have learned into action. As their leader, you should be constantly looking for teachable moments—times when you are together with the students, outside of your group time, in which you can encourage them to practice what they have been learning. Another great way to do this is to set up service projects or experiential learning times. Session five in this book provides what you need to set up one of these learning experiences.

After a few minutes, ask if there are any volunteers who would like to share some of the things they wrote down. After the volunteers have shared, discuss as a group the possibility that there are people in this world who can benefit from the negative things that have happened to us.

Before you wrap up this session, throw out a few more questions to the group: What if you run into someone who's facing a problem you've never encountered? Let's say you've never had any experience with this kind of problem. Can you still offer that person empathy? If so, how?

If your students need a hint, have someone read Romans 12:15. Then remind them of Jesus' example in John 11. Because Jesus cared so deeply for the people who were mourning Lazarus's death, He allowed their pain to become His pain. That's the model we need to learn to follow. If we truly care about

3B CUSTOM DISCIPLESHIP

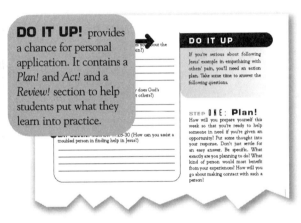

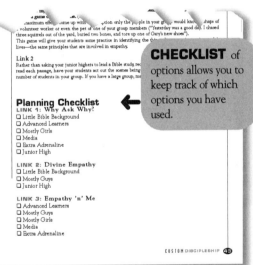

LOOK IT UP! is a section of the student journal page that encourages kids to continue their process of discipleship through the week. It provides a passage of Scripture and a question for each day of the week.

TALK IT UP! provides a place to write down personal prayer requests as well as the needs of accountability partners.

DO IT UP! provides a chance for personal application. It contains a *Plan!* and *Act!* and a *Review!* section to help students put what they learn into practice.

CHECKLIST of options allows you to keep track of which options you have used.

OPTIONS are designed for specific types of groups but provide great variety if you want to mix and match.

EACH ICON represents a type of group and designates options specific for that group.

THIS HEADING tells the section of the session where this option can be used.

Journal

HEART CHECK:
A Practical Approach to Empathy

You may think you've picked up some valuable tips for empathizing with those in need, but unless you actually put them to use in your life these tips are worthless. Remember, God wants not only "listeners" of His Word, but "does" (James 1:22). This sheet is for doers.

LOOK IT UP

Below you'll find seven Scripture references, one for every day of the week. Each passage listed below has something interesting to say about empathy for others. Spend a few minutes each day looking up the passage and writing down a few (relevant) thoughts that pop into your head.

DAY ONE: Philippians 1:29-30 (What do you think it means to "suffer" for Jesus?)

DAY TWO: Philippians 4:14 (How would you go about sharing in someone else's troubles?)

TALK IT UP

Jesus tells us that "all things are possible with God" (Mark 10:27). That includes using the pain and suffering you've experienced in your own life to help others. So when you're faced with a situation that calls for you to put some of your hard-earned life lessons to use, a wise first step is to consult the One who makes all things possible. Take some time to write down a few prayer requests, specific ways in which you need the Lord to help you empathize with others. (For example, you might ask Him to help you recognize what you have to offer certain people.) Don't be afraid to get personal here. No one else needs to see your prayer request list.

DO IT UP

If you're serious about following Jesus' example in empathizing with others' pain, you'll need an action plan. Take some time to answer the following questions.

STEP ONE: Plan!

How will you prepare yourself this week so that you're ready to help someone in need if you're given an opportunity? Put some thought into your response. Don't just settle for an easy answer. Be specific. What exactly are you planning to do? What kind of person would most benefit from your experiences? How will you go about making contact with such a person?

...maximum effect... come up with... option only the people in your group... would know... shape of... volunteer worker or even the part of one of your group members ("Yesterday was a good day. I chased three squirrels out of the yard, buried two bones, and tore up one of Gary's new shoes"). This game will give your students some practice in identifying the thi... lives—the same principles that are involved in empathy.

Link 2

Rather than asking your junior highers to lead a Bible study, rec... read each passage, have your students act out the scenes being... number of students in your group. If you have a large group, ma...

Planning Checklist

LINK 1: Why Ask Why?
- ☐ Little Bible Background
- ☐ Advanced Learners
- ☐ Mostly Girls
- ☐ Media
- ☐ Extra Adrenaline
- ☐ Junior High

LINK 2: Divine Empathy
- ☐ Little Bible Background
- ☐ Mostly Guys
- ☐ Junior High

LINK 3: Empathy 'n' Me
- ☐ Advanced Learners
- ☐ Mostly Guys
- ☐ Mostly Girls
- ☐ Media
- ☐ Extra Adrenaline

CUSTOM DISCIPLESHIP 43

Session 1 Options

LITTLE BIBLE BACKGROUND

Link 1

If your group members aren't familiar with what the Bible says about God, Resource 3A may raise more questions than it answers. If possible, go through the following Scripture passages to address some of the false claims about God on Resource 3A: (1) John 3:16; (2) Philippians 4:11-13; (3) Matthew 19:26; (4) Romans 5:12-21; (5) Psalm 33:13-15; (7) Isaiah 55:9.

Link 2

Needed: candy bar

If you're looking for a relatively quick diversion for your Bible rookies, offer a candy bar or some other incentive to the first person who can memorize John 11:35 ("Jesus wept"). Make sure your group members keep their Bibles closed until you give a signal. You might announce that the first person to find the verse, memorize it, stand up, and recite it will be declared the winner.

ADVANCED LEARNERS

Link 1

If you don't think your group members are challenged enough by your discussion of empathy, throw out a few really tough questions. Ask: **Why do you suppose God chooses to work through painful situations? Why doesn't He just work through happiness or laughter? What might He find useful about suffering?**

Link 3

Spend a few minutes concentrating on the nuts and bolts of empathy. Ask: **How would you try to convince someone who's hurting that you kind of know h... help? What things would you ... not ... why... try? If ...**

LIVE AND IN PERSON!

Key Questions
• What did it mean for Jesus to identify with and embrace the world?
• In what ways did Jesus become like us?
• How can we, as Christians, identify with and embrace the world without compromising what we believe in?

Bible Base
John 1:1, 14, 18
Philippians 2:5-8
Hebrews 4:15-16

Supplies
• Pencils
• Bibles
• Copies of Resources 1A, 1B, Journal

Opener (Optional)

Have students observe what other teens are wearing, then give them 30 seconds to pair up with a person who is dressed like them. (For example, someone wearing the same brand of jeans, similar colored T-shirts, name-brand shoes, etc.) (If you have an uneven numbers of teens, a group of three will work fine here.) After your students have found people with similar interest in clothing styles, have them attempt to find a person or group of people who share common music interests. Invite teens to shout out a style of music they enjoy, such as rock, jazz, country, alternative, contemporary Christian, R & B, hip-hop, etc., and have students with similar interests form small groups. If there are a few students who don't fit into a typical music mold, that's O.K. Allow them to be by themselves or join other people with unique musical tastes. If you want more interaction, try grouping teens by favorite foods, dream cars, types of movies, celebrities, etc.

Transition by saying, **Isn't it great when you can easily relate to someone else? Often times we think we don't have anything in common with others, but when we begin talking with them, we find out just how alike we really are. Today's lesson will help us see how Jesus identified with us by coming to earth on our behalf.**

LEARNER LINK

Don't be too surprised if some of your students laugh or make fun of those pretending to be the people in the descriptions from Resource 1A. Allow teens to enjoy this activity, but be careful the joking doesn't go too far, especially later when students begin to share about whom they most identify with. Don't allow your teens to judge others, but instead use this opportunity to help them see and celebrate the differences we all have. Remind them how boring the world would be if everyone was exactly alike!

MAKING IT REAL

For the next four or five weeks, you will be teaching your students what it means to be disciples of Jesus Christ. One of the most helpful things you can do to help them grow as disciples is to assign "accountability partners." Explain to your group members that, for the next few weeks, accountability partners will be responsible for checking on and encouraging each other's growth as disciples. The partners should plan on hooking up at least twice a week (whether at school or by phone) to update each other on their discipleship efforts.

Let's See Some Identification

Make as many photocopies of "Picture This!" (Resource 1A) as you have students. Then circle one description on each photocopied page (different descriptions for each student) before passing them out.

Tell your students that sometimes the best way to learn to identify with someone is to picture what it would be like to be that person—to be in their shoes.

Explain that they are to pretend to be the person circled on their paper. Have them talk like that person might talk, act out that person's behavior, or describe what that person might be like to the rest of the group. Give your students a few minutes to mingle but insist that they act like the person circled on their sheet during this time. After students have participated, ask:

How did you know how to act like this person? Invite your students to share how they knew how to imitate this type of person either because they've seen people like this at school or they are actually a lot like this type of person.

Do you think you understand this person? Why or why not?

What more would you need to know about this person to understand him or her better?

What is the best way to find out what this person is really like?

Did it make you uncomfortable to pretend to be this person or was it easy for you?

Would you have chosen to act like this person, or someone else, if given a choice?

Next, ask each person in the group to pick one of the people described on the sheet with whom they can best identify with or relate to. (Expect some students to introduce some humor here. Just make sure the joking doesn't get out of control or hurt others.) Ask each student to think of at least three reasons why he or she can relate to the kind of person on the sheet that he or she picked. Give some of students the opportunity to share aloud about who they picked and why they chose who they did. Take a few minutes to do this.

Ask: **Why is it that you passed over some types of people and chose the ones that you did?**

Is there anyone here you would like to be more like?

Are there any people here that you have absolutely nothing in common with and whom you would never want to be like?

Do any of the people described actually disgust you?

If so, why? (Take responses)

Share with your students that this exercise is a small attempt to help them "get into the world" of other people, to try and understand a little of who people are and what they are really like.

Point out that this session will help us better understand how Jesus got into our world. The difference being that Jesus didn't pretend; He actually became one of us.

The Ultimate Download

When we talk about how God became human, we're unraveling a mystery. Most of us know *when* and *how* it happened (the story of Christ's birth in Bethlehem), but when we stop and think how the infinite God of the universe humbled Himself to become one of us, it's a real mindblower.

Have one of your students read John 1:1, 14, 18. As a means of reviewing what they may already know, ask, **Who is "the Word" in vss. 1 and 14?** Jesus. Then ask:

What did John mean when he wrote "the Word became flesh"? He meant that God, who is spirit (unseen) and infinite (unlimited), became a human named Jesus who had flesh (seen) and in a body that was finite (limited). **This, of course, was a miracle. Can we fully understand this in our lifetime?** Probably not. **Is that okay?** Yes.

Did Jesus stop being God when He became human? Not at all. Jesus was 100% God and 100% human. He merely laid aside His majesty to come to earth, while keeping His deity (His divine attributes). God, of course, never ceased being God. Reference Philippians 2:5-7 here. Point out to students that as a human, Jesus never sinned (1 Peter 2:22). He was perfect.

According to John 1:14, what did Jesus do when He "became flesh?" He *"made His dwelling among us,"* meaning He came to be with us. The phrase literally means to *"pitch a tent."* So when God came down and became human, He "camped out" with us for a while!

Read John 1:18. What do you see in this verse that tells you what Jesus did for us? He revealed the invisible God to us. The phrase *"has made Him known"* literally means that Jesus came and *"explained"* the unexplainable God to us. Have a student look up Hebrews 1:3 and read where Jesus is called *"the exact representation of His [God's] being."* In other words, He "downloaded" God into our world!

What language did Jesus speak? He spoke the common, spoken languages of His day (Hebrew, Greek and Aramaic). He didn't come speaking some unintelligible heavenly language. He didn't use speech only the angels could understand. He spoke the language of the everyday people. Hebrews 2:17 says He *"had to be made like His brothers in every way"* so He could totally identify with us.

Have the group turn to Philippians 2:5-8. Read the verses and ask them to identify the humbling steps Christ took in becoming our Savior. You may need to help them along in this. **Jesus, who was God, became human (vs. 6). But He didn't just become any human. He became a servant (vs. 7). And not just any servant, but a humble one (vs. 8). He then humbled Himself further by becoming obedient** to the point of death (8). **But not just any death. It was a tortuous cruel death on a cross (vs. 8).** Point out here to the group the incredible difference between being the God of the universe and being tortured and killed on a cross like a common criminal. **Did Jesus have to die for us?** He volunteered Himself. He died for us because He loved us. He wanted us to be able to enjoy eternal life and have access to God the Father through Him.

Link 3

A God Who Understands
One of the biggest reasons Jesus came to earth was to relate and identify with His creation. Hand out copies of "He Can Relate to That" (Resource 1B).

Have each person look through the list of emotions and choose one or two they best identify with. Have them all look up the corresponding verses, then choose three or four students (depending on your time) to read the verses aloud. Encourage them to look up the other verses on their own when they get home.

The purpose of this exercise is to help students realize the many different ways Jesus can identify with them. After students have done this, ask if they were surprised to learn that Jesus identified with them in so many areas.

LEARNER LINK

Explain that in the next four or five weeks, you'll be asking the group to share their thoughts and feelings about people both in the Bible and in their world today. Lay down a couple of boundaries for discussion times, like: respecting others' comments, not being critical or judgmental, allowing people to freely ask questions and make honest comments. Encourage your group to create an atmosphere of acceptance, as this will help everyone experience and learn more about God.

MAKING IT R E A L

Encourage your students to share prayer requests with each other. You may want to have a specific time to do this as a group or encourage accountability partners to do it sometime during the week. Ask students to commit to praying for those requests. Encourage your students to include requests related to this session, including asking God to help group members remove the obstacles in their lives that prevent them from storing up treasures in heaven.

Explain: **God looked at the world and saw all types of people—rich, poor, young, old, fancy, plain, kind, and mean. A world full of people of different personalities and races. Yet, regardless of their differences, these people all had one thing in common—they were sinful human beings.**

Only through Jesus, God's Son, could humans receive salvation, have eternal life, and know the true way to God. "For God so loved the world that he gave his one and only Son, that whoever believes in him shall not perish but have eternal life" John 3:16.

Point out that Jesus built a bridge to all people in order to show them how much He understood them.

One way this was demonstrated was in how Jesus spoke. Jesus told stories (parables) about things that were familiar to everyday people's lives: stories about farming (Mark 4:1-20), eating fish (Luke 11:11-13), birds (Matthew 6:26), flowers (Matthew 6:28-30), friends (Luke 11:5-10) and family (Luke 15:11-32).

That doesn't sound very spiritual or "churchy," does it? We might think the Son of God would communicate in a highly intelligent, spiritual language. But Jesus chose not to speak in this way. Instead, He came down to our level instead of requiring us to come up to His. He tuned in to our frequency so that we could hear Him more clearly. He got into our world so we wouldn't have to struggle to comprehend His. Because Jesus lived on earth, He is able to identify with us and with everything we experience. He relates to us as Someone who has been here, because He has.

Hand out copies of the student journal "Heart Check: A Practical Approach to Identifying with Others" at this time. This sheet is designed to help your students dig further into the Bible on their own. It will also help them apply what they've learned to their everyday lives.

Picture This!

• **a typical teenager**—This person is O.K. looking, tries to be funny, and is dressed in an outfit that would make him or her blend in nicely as he or she walked in the mall.

• **a cowboy or cowgirl**—This person is wearing a cowboy-style hat, boots, a flannel shirt, and blue-jeans. He or she loves country music and all that goes along with the wild west!

• **an athlete**—This person is strong, fit, and muscular. This person is also very popular around campus. He or she is wearing a school jersey, sweats, and tennis shoes.

• **a classical musician**—This person is dressed nicely. He or she has a serious demeanor and carries a violin case everywhere he or she goes.

• **a scholar**—This person dresses very conservatively. He or she always has a stack of books in one hand, and a backpack full of books on his or her shoulder. This person always looks like he or she is on his or her way to class or the library and shouldn't be disturbed.

• **a person who participates in extreme sports (skydiving, handgliding, etc.)**—This person is wearing casual, comfortable clothes. This person's hair is rather long and wild and his or her vocabulary is strange and hard for the average person to understand. This person is energetic and always raring to go.

• **a famous celebrity**—This person is drop-dead gorgeous. He or she is charming, popular, dressed to a "T," and very wealthy. This person also drives a sports-car and gives quite a bit of money to charity.

• **a weirdly-dressed teen**—This person looks kind of scary to the average person. He or she wears lots of jewelry, has multiple body-piercings, wears dark-colored clothes and dark boots, and has a strange hairstyle.

He Can Relate to That

In what ways was Jesus able to identify with us and our human experiences? Look up the following Scripture passages and see some of the things that Jesus experienced.

Experience	Scripture
Tempted?	Luke 4:1-2, 13
Lonely and Rejected?	Matthew 27:46
Abandoned?	Matthew 26:36, 40
Abused?	Mark 15:16-19
Sad?	John 11:33-36
Used?	John 6:26
Stressed, Discouraged?	Matthew 26:37-38
Angry?	Mark 3:5
Tired?	John 4:6
Busy?	Mark 1:29-35, 39
Tested?	Mark 8:11
Questioned/Challenged?	Mark 11:27-28
Misunderstood?	Mark 3:21
Unappreciated?	John 4:43-44
Hated?	Mark 3:6
Ignored?	Luke 7:44-46
Lied About?	Matthew 26:59-61
Betrayed?	Matthew 26:20-25
Thirsty?	John 19:28
Hungry?	Luke 4:2
Made Fun Of?	Matthew 27:29
Forsaken, Burdened by humankinds' sins?	Matthew 27:46; 2 Corinthians 5:21

© PhotoDisc, Inc.

Does it surprise you to discover that Jesus felt and experienced some of the very same things you experience? In every circumstance we face, Jesus is able to say, "I know how you feel."

HEART CHECK:
A Practical Approach to Identifying with Others

God desires that we go far beyond just knowing about the things we've discussed in this lesson. He wants us to allow our knowledge to be practical, to let it sink into and grow out of our lives. This sheet will help us think further about identifying with others.

LOOK IT UP

Below you'll find seven Scripture references, one for each day of the week. Each passage listed below has something interesting to say about relating to others' needs. Spend a few minutes each day looking up the passage, answering the questions and writing down a few (relevant) ideas that pop into your head.

DAY ONE: Matthew 9:9-13 (How did Jesus embrace the tax collectors rather than reject them at this dinner?)

_____
_____
_____
_____

DAY TWO: John 4:28-30, 39-42 (Who might the people be in verse 28, and how did Jesus use this woman to witness to them?)

_____
_____
_____
_____

DAY THREE: Acts 2:42-47 (What are some of the things the early Christians might have had in common with one another?)

_____
_____
_____
_____

DAY FOUR: Acts 17:1-4 (Why do you think Paul made it his custom to always preach to the Jews? In what ways could he relate to them?)

_____
_____

☺ TALK IT UP

Though identifying and relating to people should never be artificial, there will always be some people with whom we have a hard time relating. Spend some time in prayer now, asking God for the wisdom to identify ways to genuinely connect with those people with whom it's hard for you to do so. Ask also for strength to reach out to those who are very different than you. Thank Jesus for identifying with you by becoming a human being.

_____
_____
_____
_____
_____
_____
_____
_____
_____
_____
_____
_____
_____
_____
_____
_____
_____
_____
_____
_____
_____

DAY FIVE: Acts 17:16-34 (How did Paul seek to relate to those who were not Jews like him?)

_____

_____

_____

_____

DAY SIX: Romans 7:15-25 (What experience do all Christians share with one another?)

_____

_____

_____

_____

DAY SEVEN: 1 Thessalonians 2:6-7 (What ways did Paul, Silas, and Timothy use to connect with those to whom they were ministering? How did they embrace people as Jesus did?)

_____

_____

_____

DO IT UP

If you're serious about identifying with others as Jesus did, then you'll need a plan of action. Here is one to follow:

STEP ONE: Plan!

What are some ways this week you can begin changing your thinking about identifying with people? What obstacles will you need to overcome? How do you plan on accomplishing this in your life? Write down the name of one person with whom you need to build a bridge of communication.

STEP TWO: Act!

Put your plan into practice. Go to the person with whom you need to build a bridge of communication and attempt to talk to him or her. If you're worried about taking a direct approach, try sending an E-mail, calling that person, or dropping a note in the mail to him or her. How did that person respond to you? Will it take you more time than expected to accomplish this? Are you encouraged by your efforts so far to reach out to him or her? Why or why not?

STEP THREE: Review!

Are you glad you took these steps to improve in this area of your life? What have you learned about yourself through this process? Is there anything you will (or could) do differently or change as a result of this experience?

LITTLE BIBLE BACKGROUND

Link 2

Have your students read Romans 8:3 and Hebrews 2:14-18. Point out that Jesus took the first step in coming to us. He knew we would never be able to be made righteous on our own, so because of His love, Jesus became one of us. He spoke our language, ate our food, slept on our floors, grew weary, wept, and hurt like we do. He even looked like us, like a common person (Isaiah 53:2). He "blended in" and yet stood out at the same time. He was like us. He felt what we feel. He embraced us by identifying with us. He did this so that He could build bridges to us. **As a result, what should our response be like to Him according to Hebrews 4:15-16?**

Link 3

Jesus identified with the world without compromising any of His beliefs or moral standards (Hebrews 7:25; 1 Peter 2:22). **So what about us? How can we identify with those in the world without compromising our faith?** We must be in the world and around unbelievers, but we must also live holy lives. **What is the balance? Where are the boundaries? Where do we find that common ground with those who don't know Christ?** Your students don't have to be like those in the world to relate to them. Encourage them to always be themselves but look for common ground with others. Jesus came not to build walls between Himself and the world, but to build a bridge. Because He did this, we can too, because He lives in us.

ADVANCED LEARNERS

Link 2

Look up 1 John 2:15-17 as a group. Ask students to find from these verses the three different ways the world is described. Discuss what each of these phrases means—the cravings of sinful man, the lust of his eyes, the boasting of what he has and does. Ask how these things impact the areas of our lives, such as: the music we listen to, what types of clothes we wear, how we view sex, our material possessions, our morals, and our values. Challenge your teens to come up with a group definition of what they think it means to "love the world."

Link 3

Ask your students this question, **What are some of the differences between a Christian and a non-Christian?** See how many different things they list. Their answers may include: having different desires, hopes, dreams, activities, interests, destinies, priorities, values, morals, pursuits, and friends. **What similarities might you have with non-Christians?** Point out that Christians can actually have many things in common with non-Christians. Things like: playing on the same sports teams, listening to the same kinds of music, working the same jobs, being in the same classes, enjoying the same hobbies, wearing the same kinds of clothes, sharing the same friendships, liking the same kinds of foods, being in the same clubs, etc.

MOSTLY GUYS

Link 1

Ask, **Who is your favorite professional athlete or actor?** Then see if your guys can explain what it is about this person that they would like to imitate. Or ask, **If you could meet this person, on what common ground would you choose to try and relate? What would you say? Would you be nervous? Why or why not?**

Link 2

Have students pick a group of people they have absolutely nothing in common with or that they don't like. This group can be based on religion, school, economic status, cliques, etc. Say, **If God asked you to hang out out with these people for a month or two, what would be some of the struggles you would face? During that time, which of the following might be a temptation for you:** Pride? Prejudice? Hate? Stress? Disgust? Fear? Loneliness? Insecurity? **Imagine how Jesus must have felt, being holy and without sin, to come to this earth and live among sinners like us. But He did it anyway because He wanted to save us.**

MOSTLY GIRLS

Link 2

Ask volunteers to describe their last family vacation. How long it took to get to their final destination, whether or not they enjoyed the journey, if all the traveling was worth it, and how their destination differed from home. After giving time to share, ask them to try and imagine the distance Jesus traveled to come to earth. **Jesus left Heaven to clothe Himself in common things! But it was what awaited for Him in heaven that made it worth the trip. And what was waiting for Him there?** See Hebrews 12:2 and Philippians 2:9-11. What awaited Him was being crowned "Lord of All" and taking His seat at His Father's right hand.

Link 3

Ask the girls if they can think of someone (preferably another girl) at their school who doesn't seem to have many friends. (If the girls in your group attend the same school have them refrain from using the person's name.) Maybe this person is shy or perhaps struggles with her self-esteem. Or maybe she's just "different." Once they all have an image of this girl in their minds, ask, **What steps would someone have to take in order to reach out to this person and be her friend?** Discuss this for as long as time allows. Ask, **Would you be willing to take those steps yourself?**

MEDIA

Link 2

Needed: Video, TV/VCR

Show a short video clip from the "Jesus of Nazareth" film by Franco Zefferelli, using the scene that portrays His birth (video programming numbers 43:00—51:55 begin with Joseph and Mary going to Bethlehem and end where the shepherds visit Jesus.) Ask your students to imagine the God of the universe as a baby—helpless, and totally dependent upon His creation. **If you could ask God anything about this mysterious event, what would it be? What is there about God becoming human that is unclear to you?** Encourage your students to verbalize their questions.

Link 3

Needed: CD, CD player

Set up a tape or CD player and play the song "Mary Did You Know?" by Michael English for your group. Ask your group to try and put themselves in Mary's (or Joseph's) place at that time. **What thoughts might be filling Mary and Joseph's minds? What emotions might he or she be feeling? What unanswered questions might Mary and Joseph want to ask?** If you'd like to try a different approach, ask the group to imagine what it might have been like to be friends with Joseph and Mary at this time. Would your students have believed Mary and Joseph's story about baby Jesus?

EXTRA ADRENALINE

Link 2

Choose a large variety of famous people's names and write them down on paper. These names could range from celebrities, to famous politicians, presidents, kings and queens, even well-known staff members from your church. After arranging the group in a circle, explain that you're going to call out a name and that for 30 seconds, each group member must try to come up with a two word description that portrays who this person is. Tell them that the idea is to move as fast as they can around the circle. The first person to "draw a blank" is out, making the group smaller. Each time someone gets out, start with a new celebrity.

After the last two people play and a winner is revealed, explain that in order to win at this game, you must know something about the person being described. This means spending time watching this person, reading about this person, listening to this person or hearing about this person. The point of this activity is to show us that God didn't come to earth *just* to identify with us, but to let us learn something about Him. (See John 1:14.)

Link 3

Have your group members take off their shoes. Toss all shoes into a pile in the middle of the group. On the count of three, have everyone grab two different shoes (not their own). Your students must try to put them on as quickly as they can. Then ask, **What can you understand about the person who wears these shoes?** Be prepared for some funny responses. **Was it hard for your feet to "relate" to their shoes? Were any of them an easy fit?** Use this as a way to talk about relating to people who are different from us.

JUNIOR HIGH

Link 1

Ask the group to share if they have ever been to a costume party, been in a play, or been a part of a drama team. If no one responds to this, ask if they ever pretended to be someone else when they were little kids (like a super hero or an athlete). Find out what character they pretended to be. See if any of them wore costumes or dressed up in a special way. If any have been in a play, ask if they did anything special to prepare themselves for the role. Relate this to Jesus coming to earth to become a human. The only difference was that He wasn't pretending. He actually became one of us.

Link 2

Ask your students to imagine themselves in the following situation: You're at the mall having fun. Most of your friends are there, but there are also people you don't know very well. Unexpectedly, a few kids show up with alcohol and tell everyone they'll share it with whomever wants it. They begin heading outside to drink it. Some of your friends go with them. **Do you: Go along, drink the alcohol, and try to blend in? Politely refuse and stay at the mall? Refuse to go along with them, then call your parents? Refuse the drinks, but watch them drink?** Ask, **Is there a way to continue being friends but not drink with them? If so, how? What is the balance between relating to them and rejecting them?** Note: Mention that underage drinking is always wrong and in these kinds of situations, it is best to notify an adult. Stress that relating to these kids and doing the right thing aren't one and the same.

Planning Checklist

LINK 1: Let's See Some Identification
❑ Mostly Guys
❑ Junior High

LINK 2: The Ultimate Download
❑ Little Bible Background
❑ Advanced Learners
❑ Mostly Guys
❑ Mostly Girls
❑ Media
❑ Extra Adrenaline
❑ Junior High

LINK 3: A God Who Understands
❑ Little Bible Background
❑ Advanced Learners
❑ Mostly Girls
❑ Media
❑ Extra Adrenaline

TOTAL ACCEPTANCE... NO EXCEPTIONS

Key Questions
• How did Jesus treat sinners?
• What was His attitude towards them?
• How can we communicate Jesus' unconditional acceptance and love to people without tolerating their sins?

Bible Base
Matthew 9:9-13; 11:28-30
Luke 7:36-50
John 8:1-11

Supplies
• Pencils
• Bibles
• Copies of Resources 2A, 2B, Journal
• Paper
• Pens

Opener (Optional)
Bring a variety of snacks to your group time. Include some favorites that you know everyone will like, but throw some strange ones into the selection as well. You might include some of the following: wrapped chocolate candies, popcorn, peanuts, carrots, coffee beans, yogurt, a teaspoon of peanut butter, pieces of cereal, bouillon cubes, broccoli, etc. Spread these items out on a table and invite kids to nibble on them at the start of your time together.

LEARNER LINK
Be aware that some of your students have struggled with acceptance in their own lives. Their devastating experiences may still be with them. Some of your students may have been the victims of conditional acceptance at home (based on their grades, behaviors, or performance in sports or academics). Because of this, they may struggle in their understanding of God's unconditional acceptance of them. By communicating acceptance of them in your group time (and beyond), you will go a long way in helping them accept themselves as God does.

After having these snacks and just hanging out, draw everyone's attention to the items largely left untouched. Ask **Why didn't you choose to sample these particular "snacks?" What was it about them that made you pass them over?**

Explain that the undesirable snacks were placed there for a reason. To help members of your group better understand what they'll be studying this lesson; How Jesus Christ chose to accept people, no matter how undesirable they were.

MAKING IT REAL
Introduce your group members to the art of journaling. Ask your students to keep a journal or diary of their observations, feelings, and frustrations as they take steps each day to be a more devoted disciple of Jesus Christ. Encourage them to be consistent in writing in their journals. Point out that journaling may be difficult at first, but that the more they do it, the better they will become. Furthermore, the better they become, the more they will benefit from it.

Link 1

Not Making the Grade

Begin by reviewing the "Heart Check: A Practical Approach to Identifying with Others" from last session. Then pass out copies of "Conditions for Use" (Resource 2A) to your students. Give students a few minutes to jot down their responses to five or six of the circumstances described on the sheet. Next go around the group and ask students to share their answers. Ask, **Have any of these things ever happened to you personally?** Allow those who are willing, to share their experiences with the group. Here are some questions related to the handout that might help you get started.

How did it make you feel when you were rejected when . . . [refer to one of the choices offered on the sheet]? They are listed below.

• You aren't accepted as a member of the National Honor Society because your grades aren't considered good enough.

• You aren't received by the hospital in the emergency room because . . .

• You don't make the team because . . .

• You aren't hired for the job because . . .

• You can't get a date with that guy or girl because . . .

• You can't get approval from your parents because . . .

• You aren't the teacher's favorite because . . .

• You don't get an award at school because . . .

• The leader points you out as a bad example during a youth group meeting because . . .

• You get cut from the band because . . .

• You look in the mirror and frown because . . .

• The "in" crowd rejects you because . . .

• You are made fun of in your school because . . .

Have any of you ever been in a situation where you didn't feel accepted? Share about it with us.

How was that rejection communicated to you? Through words? Or in another way?

How does that experience still affect you today?

All of the examples from Resource 2A are how our world bases acceptance of others on external standards or behavior. Again, not all of them are morally wrong. However, they do communicate the mindset of conditional acceptance. Sometimes we take that worldly way of thinking and transfer it over into our relationship with God. This isn't right, because God loves and accepts us unconditionally. Although God hates our sin, he never hates us.

Link 2

Jesus' Open Arms Policy

One of the things about Jesus which made Him unique was how He treated people. One thing He made perfectly clear to those around Him was that there would be no list of conditions placed on people. They would be unconditionally loved by him. Discuss with your group the following three scenes from the life of Jesus to help them get a big picture of how He received people unconditionally.

Scene #1—A Dinner with Sinners (Matthew 9:9-13)
Who was present at this party? Five different groups:

• Matthew, a tax-collector (vss. 9-10)—a tax gatherer might be a modern-equivalent of an IRS agent, only the tax collector in Jesus' day would have had a reputation for cheating people and being very dishonest.

• Many other tax-gatherers (vs. 10)—These were Matthew's buddies and fellow cheaters.

• The "Sinners" (vs. 10)—people whose sinful lifestyles made them unacceptable to the self-righteous Jewish leaders.

• The Pharisees (vs. 11)—men who had lots of rules for being righteous and placed numerous conditions on people.

• Jesus and His disciples (vs. 10).

Imagine such a diverse group of people gathered together for one meal! What problem did the Pharisees have with Jesus being in this kind of group? They were appalled that He was having dinner with sinners. **What do you think was wrong with that in their eyes?** They believed that being spiritual and holy meant not having contact with sinful people, whom they considered "unclean." Jesus challenged the Pharisees' belief system by eating with these people and accepting them. In fact, verse 10 indicates that Jesus was right in the middle of them.

Do you see any evidence here that these sinners had a problem eating with the Pharisees? No, though they may have felt uncomfortable, there is no indication of them not accepting the Pharisees.

Isn't it interesting that many times "sinners" accept one another better than "religious" people do? **How did Jesus justify His presence with those people?** Jesus said He had come to help those who were sick with sin, not those who "had it all together" (vss. 12-13).

Scene #2—Nobody Gets Left Out (Matthew 11:28-30)
Who does Jesus extend this invitation to? He offers it to all people (vs. 28). **What does Jesus promise those who come to Him?** Rest (vs. 28). **Rest from what?** Rest from the heavy burden of laws the Pharisees had placed on the backs of the people. Those in the religious establishment had made up hundreds of requirements for people to meet in order to be right with God. As a result, people viewed their acceptance by God as conditional and based only on how many laws they could keep. But Jesus says here that He accepts all who come, and that His demands on our lives are not a burden (vss. 29-30).

Scene #3—A Lesson in Forgiveness (Luke 7:36-50)
This time Jesus was having dinner at the house of a Pharisee. A certain woman heard that Jesus was there and decided to "crash" the party. How is this woman described in verse 37? She is called a sinner. We don't know who this woman was, but it is possible she was a prostitute. If this was the case, then it must have been quite a shock for her to show up. **What does she do to Jesus (vs. 38)?** We find her at His feet (a sign of humility), weeping. Her tears are flowing down her cheeks and onto Jesus' feet. She wipes her tears off of His feet with her hair and kisses Jesus' feet as well.

How did the Pharisee who invited Jesus to his house respond to this (vs. 39)? He thought Jesus must not be who He claimed to be, or else He would know who this woman was and would not allow here to do this. Ask, **What would you say is the modern-day teenage equivalent to this woman?** Maybe a drug user or someone who is promiscuous or a known "party-er." **How do you think your church, youth group or Bible study group would respond to a person like this if she showed up for a Bible study?**

Jesus calls this Pharisee by name and responds to him. How? By telling him a short story about a debt that was forgiven (41-42). **What was the point of Jesus' story (vs. 47)?** That great love for God flows out of a heart that realizes how much it has been forgiven. Instead of rejecting and rebuking this woman, Jesus accepted her completely and praised her publicly (vss. 44-46). Her sins were forgiven (vs. 48), then He sent her on her way (vs. 50).

Bottom Line: Jesus accepts sinners when no one else will. He places no conditions on His acceptance either. This doesn't mean Jesus accepts the sins people commit, but He is willing to love people regardless of their sins. Jesus wants people to confess their sins and seek Jesus for salvation.

Link 3

The Feeling of Acceptance
Pass out copies of "Acting Out Acceptance"(Resource 2B) and play out the drama portrayed in it. After doing this, ask your group, **What do you think was going through the mind of this woman?** Encourage them to try and place themselves in her position. Jesus literally had the power of life and death in His words. His response to the Pharisees could have sentenced her to a very painful death (stoning). **How do you think she felt when she realized that Jesus wasn't going to condemn her?** She may have been thinking, *No one has ever shown this kind of love to me before. No one has ever accepted me because I am a sinner— certainly not the religious crowd. Maybe this Jesus is who He says He is. Maybe God does love me after all.*

Keep in mind that some students will tend to talk more than others. In fact, one or two may tend to dominate most discussions. Be sensitive to this and keep balance in your group by remembering the following things: The questions contained in the study are not meant to evoke a yes or no response, but to stimulate discussion. By asking open-ended questions, you allow a variety of responses. Next, call on your students by name. This gives everyone a chance to make a contribution to the group. It also helps those who may be a little more reserved to open up. You may also want to consider making a "rule" that each person only gets one response per question (or at least until everyone has had a chance to talk). That way they won't be able to "hog" the discussion. Finally, be sure and praise the responses of your students, even if they don't always get the "right" answer. This encourages them to speak up without fear of rejection or ridicule. In that way, you are also communicating and modeling loving acceptance to them.

MAKING IT REAL

Some of your students may have needs that don't get addressed during your group time. Make a special effort to get to know all of your student's individually. That may mean a phone call or a trip to a sporting event or a lunch together. Not only will this help you build relationships with the students, but seeing you outside of your discipleship group will help them connect what they learn to their everyday lives.

What is the difference between the way Jesus accepts sinners and the way other sinners accept each other? Get your group to discuss this and brainstorm about this for a while. Point out that those who live in sin tend to accept the behavior of one a other, while Jesus rejects the sinful behavior but still accepts the person.

Conclude by reminding your students that how Jesus embraced people is something that we can strive to do in our lives as well. As we embrace those that aren't easy to love, Jesus' love will show forth in our lives. It's easy to love the loveable people, what made Jesus so unique was that he loved and embraced the unlovable. That is also what made the biggest impact on the world.

Hand out copies of the student journal "Heart Check: A Practical Approach to Accepting Others" and encourage your students to look up the Scriptures and apply these principles of embracing the world as Jesus did.

Conditions for Use

Everywhere we look in our society, we are faced with conditions that other people place upon us. While not all of these are necessarily bad in themselves, they do tell us that there aren't many places or circumstances where we are accepted as we are—no questions asked. Look at the following scenarios and try to come up with conditions for acceptance that might apply to them. For example,

You aren't accepted as a member of the National Honor Society because your grades aren't considered good enough.

You aren't received by the hospital in the emergency room because . . .

You don't make the team because . . .

You aren't hired for the job because . . .

You can't get a date with that guy or girl because . . .

You can't get approval from your parents because . . .

You aren't the teacher's favorite because . . .

You don't get an award at school because . . .

The leader points you out as a bad example during a youth group meeting because . . .

You get cut from the band because . . .

You look in the mirror and frown because . . .

The "in" crowd rejects you because . . .

You are made fun of in your school because . . .

Acting Out Acceptance

Narrator
Jesus
Scribes and Pharisees (can be as few as two people)
The Woman caught in adultery
The Disciples
The Crowd

Narrator: *The scene opens with Jesus teaching the people and His disciples (have "Jesus" reading from Matthew 5—The Sermon on the Mount).* **The crowd and the disciples are gathered around Jesus at His feet. While teaching the people, suddenly there is a commotion and Jesus is interrupted. The Scribes and Pharisees bring a woman to Jesus and make her stand in front of the crowd. The woman hangs her head low, burying her face in her hands.**

Scribes and Pharisees: Teacher, this woman has been caught in the act of adultery. In the Law, Moses commanded us to stone such women. What do you say we do with her? *Look at each other, then whisper,* **We've got Him now. He's trapped. We'll use His answer to accuse Him of breaking the Law. Then we can have Him arrested and we'll be done with this troublemaker.**

Jesus: *Almost as if He is ignoring them, bends down and begins to draw on the ground with His finger.*

Scribes and Pharisees: Answer us, teacher! What should we do with her? Tell us!

Jesus: *Stands up abruptly and brushes the dirt off His hands. Then says,* **If any one of you is without sin, let him be the first to throw a stone at her.** *He then stoops and begins writing again.*

Scribes and Pharisees: *Look again at each another, then walk away from the scene one by one.*

Jesus: *Stands and says,* **Woman, where are they? Has no one condemned you?**

Woman: No one, sir.

Jesus: Then neither do I condemn you. Go now and leave your life of sin.

Narrator: *The woman gives Jesus a smile of gratitude, turns, and walks away.*

HEART CHECK:
A Practical Approach to Accepting Others

God desires that we go far beyond just knowing about the things we've discussed in this lesson. He wants us to allow our knowledge to be practical, to let it sink into and grow out of our lives. This section will help us think further about accepting others.

LOOK IT UP

Below you'll find seven Scripture references, one for each day of the week. Each passage listed below has something interesting to say about accepting others. Spend a few minutes each day looking up the passage and writing down a few (relevant) ideas that pop into your head.

DAY ONE: Philemon 1-21 (What does this short story tell you about accepting one another?)

_____
_____
_____
_____

DAY TWO: Acts 2:41-47 (What do you see in the early church that made all those people get along in spite of their great differences?)

_____
_____
_____
_____

DAY THREE: Acts 8:26-40 (What obstacles might Philip have had to overcome in order to reach out to this Ethiopian?)

_____
_____
_____
_____

DAY FOUR: Acts 9:11-19 (On what basis was Ananias able to fully accept Saul of Tarsus?)

_____
_____
_____

☺ TALK IT UP

Talking about accepting others is easy. Anyone can do that. But actually living it out is another story. You may have some struggles accepting certain people in your life right now. That's O.K., because we all struggle that way. But one key is to talk about these struggles with the Lord. Make a personal list of the people you have a hard time accepting unconditionally. Pray through those names one-by-one, mentioning them to God and telling Him what it is that bothers you about these people. Ask Him to help you see the sins you struggle with now, and/or the wrongs you did to others before you became a Christian. Then ask the Lord to help you accept others as He has accepted you.

_____
_____
_____
_____
_____
_____
_____
_____
_____
_____
_____
_____
_____
_____
_____
_____
_____
_____
_____

DAY FIVE: Galatians 6:1-5 (What do you see in these verses that helps you receive others in spite of their faults and failures? What might it mean to fulfill the law of Christ?)

_____

_____

_____

DAY SIX: John 20:26-29 (Compare and contrast Jesus' acceptance of Thomas with Thomas acceptance of Jesus. What conditions do you see here?)

_____

_____

_____

_____

DAY SEVEN: Ephesians 2:1-10 (What can you discover in this passage about Jesus' unconditional acceptance of you?)

_____

_____

_____

_____

DO IT UP

If you're serious about accepting the world as Jesus did, then you'll need an action plan. Here is one to follow:

STEP ONE: **Plan!**

Write down the conditions you tend to place on others. Do this by taking a sheet of paper and writing down the following phrase 10 times: "I easily accept people who . . . .". Then complete as many of those 10 sentences as you can. Don't rush through this—really think about it.

STEP TWO: **Act!**

Now go back through that list again and put it together with the names you wrote down in your prayer list. See how many sentences you can match up with a name. Some names may appear more than once. Then ask yourself how God might have you work through each of those conditions of acceptance. How will you eliminate those conditions from your relationships? What specific steps will you take?

STEP THREE: **Review!**

Were you able to put some of those steps into action? How did your "difficult people" respond? What did you discover or learn about yourself? In what ways was this a growing experience for you?

LITTLE BIBLE BACHGROUND

Link 2

The "yoke" Jesus spoke of in Matthew 11:29 refers to a wooden "m"-shaped device placed on oxen and used for farming. A plow was attached to the yoke and the oxen would pull it. This yoke was large and heavy and would wear on the neck of the animals, causing them to develop sores and calluses. It wasn't a privilege to be harnessed to a yoke. It was work. The farmers would also use the yoke to control the oxen. They would pull on the reins to guide them or to make them stop. But Jesus' explained that His "yoke" wouldn't be a burden. He is a gentle Master (vs. 29). His yoke is to help us rest.

Link 3

Scribes were professional scholars who taught the people the Law of God. The were known for making a mountain out of a molehill. The Pharisees were also very "religious." They enjoyed wearing religious clothing and being recognized for being spiritual. Everything they did focused on outward duty and ritual, but rarely, if ever, did they focus on the hearts of others or their own faults. They loved tradition more than God (Mark 7:1-13) and prided themselves on their legalism. Jesus denounced both groups for their pride and their rigid, cold, and uncaring lifestyles (Matthew 23).

ADVANCED LEARNERS

Link 2

As you study these passages, think about this: Jesus accepts us as we are because He knows that we are powerless to change ourselves. It makes sense then for us to accept non-Christians where they are because any attempt to change themselves won't help them get closer to God. It doesn't mean we agree with what they're doing anymore than Jesus approves of their sin. It just means we recognize that only Christ has the power to save and change a person. Jesus never said to anyone, Go and clean–up your life. Get it all together and them come back to me. He promised, "Whoever comes to Me I will never drive away" (John 6:37).

Link 3

What do you think accepting another person really communicates? Would you agree or disagree with the following statement: Christians often don't accept "sinners" unconditionally because they are concerned that the sinners won't see their sins unless they are pointed out to them. As students share, mention that most people know they are sinners, but most don't know they are loved. Often times the persistent love shown to them by Christians is what helps lead them to Christ. **What are some of the reasons we are so quick to condemn and so slow to accept?** Allow your group to openly communicate here about some of their frustrations about this topic. Intervene gently if the discussion gets too heated.

MOSTLY GUYS

Link 2

Ask your guys if they think pride is a factor that could keep them from accepting others. **Do they think it is harder for guys to accept unlikeable people? Or for girls?** There is no right or wrong answer here. Only opinions. **What is it about a prideful person that makes him or her exclude others? Do you think this is a sin or just a personal weakness? What's the difference?** Invite your guys to open up here about some of the prideful struggles they may face.

Link 3

Who has been instrumental in your life in teaching you about what it means to accept others? Allow various guys to share about this person here. **How did this person communicate acceptance to you? How did this person use his or her words? Actions? Time? Money? Gifts? Did he or she ever**

actually say, "I accept you"? How are you different because of this person's influence in your life? (You may want to ask these questions one at a time, or ask them continually as one of your guys is sharing.)

MOSTLY GIRLS

Link 1

After participating in the exercise found in Resource 2A, tell the group that some people think that God accepts us only if we meet certain conditions. **What might some of those conditions be?** Allow the girls to share here. **Do you agree or disagree?** Again, allow interaction. **Do you think how people view God affects the way they look at themselves or other people? If so, in what way is this true? And if a girl has trouble believing God accepts her, how will that affect the way she accepts others?** Invite your girls to share here about an experience they may have had with a person who didn't accept himself or herself. Then ask your girls how they might help these kinds of people.

Link 3

Ask group members how easy or difficult the people in the following list would be to personally accept into their youth group. See if you can make a "Top Ten" list, concluding with the most difficult one of all to accept: Kristi who is a drug user; Dan who sleeps around; Kevin who cusses a lot; Brent who laughs at Christians; Katie who is a snob; Missy who rarely comes to youth group or church but is friendly at school; John who has body odor; Melissa who comes from a very poor family; Chris who lies a lot; Cathy who is hateful to others; Max who plays mean practical jokes on people

MEDIA

Link 2

Needed: CD, CD player

Play the song "The Invitation" from Steven Curtis Chapman's *Speechless* CD. **What do you hear about God's acceptance of us that makes us speechless? What's amazing about seeing His arms open wide to receive us? Is it hard or easy for you to picture God this way?** Explain your answer.

Link 3

Needed: CD, CD player

Play dc Talk's "Colored People" (or better yet, show the video). Discuss the effect that race, skin color, background, and religion have on our treatment of one another. **How has prejudice and discrimination changed our world? What would you say are the most important steps to overcoming these barriers?** Some examples to share with your students might be: praying for people, being open-minded, befriending people of many races and backgrounds, putting themselves in other people's shoes, etc.

EXTRA ADRENALINE

Link 1

Get your students to play the following body language game. Take the list of phrases below and have students communicate each phrase without saying a word. Take two volunteers for each phrase. Each person must stand up, use only their bodies (eyes, mouth, face, arms) without making a sound. Here are the phrases: **I love you. Where have you been? It's cold and wet outside. What's that smell? Do you know great you are? I'm upset with you. Where's my new CD? He's (she's) so fine! I can't understand calculus! This food is gross! Thank you. I love being here with all of you! I have no money whatsoever. I was on my computer last night until midnight!** Use this fun exercise to point out that we can communicate many things in life without ever speaking a word. We can even say, "I accept you" without talking. Ask the group **What are some ways we could do that without actually saying it?**

Link 3

Tell students you're going to form a club. The purpose of the club is to be as exclusive as possible. You want to keep out as many people as you can and only have members who share similar interests. Have everyone write down a condition for club membership on a piece of paper and turn it in (for example, all members must like chocolate or play an instrument to join). Then have them turn in the slips of paper to you and proceed to read them to the group. Since all club members must meet all requirements, see how many "members" there actually are by the time you read all the slips of paper. **Did anyone meet all the requirements?** Use this exercise to help students see that the more conditions we place on people, the less chance we have for a relationship with them.

JUNIOR HIGH

Link 1
Have two people roleplay the following scenario (one answers the phone, the other is the caller): **Tonight when you get home, the phone rings. It's a person from your school but he or she is not someone you'd call a "friend." He or she moved to your town three months ago. The conversations starts like this, "We're in English class but I'm not sure if we've talked. I was wondering if you'd like to meet me at the mall and catch a movie? I got some free movie tickets but didn't want to go by myself . . ."** Allow various groups of students to act this out. Then discuss the following question as a large group: **How could you show God's love to him or her?**

Link 2
Give this test to your junior highers. 1. There's a girl in youth group who has a horrible reputation at school. You should: a. avoid her; b. tell her to straighten up her life; c. ask her to lead the next Bible study; d. see if she wants to join the rest of you for pizza after church.

2. James keeps disrupting the Bible study, throwing things at people and making gross noises. To show him that you accept him, but not his behavior, you should: a. throw stuff back at him; b. take him out back and leave him there; c. shout Bible verses at him; d. tell him you want him to join in the discussion, but he'll have to leave if he can't listen thoughtfully to everyone else's ideas.

3. An elderly person says to you, "God loves good little boys and girls, so be good." That statement makes you: a. want to be good; b. confused because you thought it was the sinners He really loves; c. mad because this person seems so clueless. You aren't little and don't like being treated that way; d. smile, because you know this person is just trying to be friendly.

Planning Checklist

LINK 1: Not Making the Grade
- ❏ Mostly Girls
- ❏ Extra Adrenaline
- ❏ Junior High

LINK 2: Jesus' Open Arms Policy
- ❏ Little Bible Background
- ❏ Advanced Learners
- ❏ Mostly Guys
- ❏ Media
- ❏ Junior High

LINK 3: The Feeling of Acceptance
- ❏ Little Bible Background
- ❏ Advanced Learners
- ❏ Mostly Guys
- ❏ Mostly Girls
- ❏ Media
- ❏ Extra Adrenaline

JESUS EXPERIENCED THINGS YOU DO

Key Questions

- How did Jesus show people He genuinely cared about them?
- What does Jesus' compassion reveal to us about the heart of God?
- How can we touch people with care and compassion?

Bible Base

Mark 1:40-45; 6:34
Matthew 15:30-31

Supplies

- Pencils
- Bible
- Copies of Resources 3A, 3B, Journal
- dictionary (optional)
- Newspaper (Opener)

Opener (Optional)

Needed: Newspaper

Ahead of time, get a current copy of your local newspaper (or a national newspaper) and go through it. Highlight every article that deals in some way with human suffering. Some areas you might highlight could include: earthquakes, wars, floods, divorces, labor disputes, lawsuits, obituaries, shootings, burglaries, murders, arrests, even athletes' injuries. You may want to choose a short, specific article and read it in its entirety, but look for anything you can find that relates to how people are experiencing difficult times. Consider asking a student to read the article aloud. After reading those headlines (or an excerpt from an article), ask your students:

What were you thinking as you heard what these people were going through? What did you honestly feel inside? Indifference? Relief or thankfulness that it wasn't you? Sorrow? Sadness? Hurt? Regret? Anger? Have you ever experienced a similar situation? Allow students to share. **What is it about their situation that affects you the most? Is there anything you can personally do to relieve any of this suffering? If not, how does that make you feel?** Allow various students to respond to these questions.

LEARNER LINK

Take a few minutes at the beginning of each study to give your students an overview (or preview) of what you're going to discuss in the lesson. Based on the application later on in the lesson, highlight two or three benefits they will receive from this study. One of your goals as leader is to do what you can to help your students remember what they've learned. You can accomplish this by: being excited about the lesson yourself, helping them see God's truth demonstrated to them in the verses they look up in their Bibles, allowing them to discuss as much as possible, and by using illustrations and applications that get them involved in the learning process (such as the activities and options suggested in each lesson).

MAKING IT REAL

As you get to know your students better, pray for them specifically. Taking the time to do this will help you focus on their needs. It will also help you to continually acknowledge and trust that it is God who is making these students into disciples of Jesus Christ—sometimes even in spite of your efforts.

Link 1

The Heartbeat of God

Review the student journal "Heart Check: A Practical Approach to Accepting Others" from last week.

You've already discussed together what it meant for Jesus to identify with the world and to accept sinners as they are. In this lesson you're taking the group a step further by looking at how Jesus became even more involved with us by actually feeling our pain. Ask the group, **What comes to your mind when you think of the word "compassion?" What does it mean to truly care about somebody?** Discuss this for a few minutes.

Challenge the group to see if they can see Jesus' compassion in the following verses:

Mark 5:25-34   Jesus has compassion on a woman who has been sick for 12 years. **Why did He choose her?**

Luke 19:41   Jesus wept over Jerusalem because it didn't accept Him as Messiah. **What background information do you know about Jerusalem that might help you understand why Jesus felt this way?**

Luke 23:34   Jesus showed compassion to those who were crucifying Him. **How could He possibly have cared so much about these people?**

In what way was being compassionate a big part of Jesus' earthly mission? How did it contribute to His overall objective? His compassion in specific circumstances served to illustrate the compassion he would later demonstrate on the cross as He died for undeserving sinners.

Ask the group to list as many attributes (characteristics) of God as they can. Answers might include: all-knowing, all-powerful, ever-present, loving, righteous, holy, just, sovereign, unchanging, infinite, and eternal. **How does compassion reveal the character and heart of God to us?** Look at Isaiah 1:18; 45:22; and Revelation 22:17. **What do these verses tell you about who God really is?** They tell us that the heart of God longs to reach out to undeserving creatures like us, to redeem us. **God wants a relationship with us. That is hard to conceive, but it is true.**

Link 2

Jesus Meets the Untouchable

Turn to Mark 1:40-45. Make sure everyone has found the passage before you ask a group member to read it out loud. Since it's true that a picture is worth a thousand words, ask your students to try and imagine this scene in their minds (like watching a video in their imagination).

This man came to Jesus in reverence, humility and faith (vs. 41). Notice how Jesus responded. Ask, **What do you think it means to feel compassion for someone?** Answers might range from feeling sorry for a person to actually shedding tears of sorrow. Consider bringing a dictionary and asking a student to look up the word in the dictionary. Use the "Advanced Learning" section for the biblical meaning of compassion at this point.

This man's condition deeply affected Jesus. It impacted Him in a great way. Again, challenge your students to imagine themselves present at this scene. **Describe the look you see on Jesus' face. Could it be possible that His eyes were filled with tears?** Imagine the hopelessness of a man with leprosy in that day. Refer to the section "Little Bible Background" for some information on what it was like for someone to have the disease of leprosy in Jesus' day.

What did the compassion inside Jesus cause Him to do next in vs. 41? He reached out His hand and touched him. **Why was this such a radical thing to do?** Because in that day leprosy was thought to be communicated through physical touch. **How do you think the crowd reacted? How do you imagine the disciples responded?** There was probably a huge gasp that rippled throughout the crowd, their faces frozen in shock. How unexpected this touch must have been to those standing there that day.

What do you think Jesus' touch here was like? It wasn't a touch like touching a hot iron to see if it's hot. Jesus cared about him when it wasn't convenient or popular. **Try and imagine how long it had been since this man had felt the touch of another human being. Months, years, possibly over a decade? Did he have a family? How long since he had kissed his wife? Held his children? Felt the warm handshake of a friend? Picture the loneliness he must have experienced. What it felt like being branded as "unclean," unwanted, untouchable.**

But Jesus changed all that with one touch of compassion. Notice in vs. 41 that Jesus wanted this man to know that He was willing to make him clean. In fact, Jesus desired to heal this man more than the leper desired to be healed. And as vss. 41-42 tell us, He spoke the word and the man was instantly made whole. The leprosy just disappeared. Limbs, fingers, lips—all were made brand new. Better than brand new. It was a miracle, something only God could have done. His cleansing was immediate and complete. Nothing was left unclean. Not a spot or trace of the horrible disease of leprosy was left anywhere on him. And his cleansing was visible to everyone around him. No one could dispute or argue with the reality of the change. And it was a permanent change, too. That's what Christ's compassion and care did for this poor leper.

Can you see this man's eyes opening as wide as saucers as he sees his hands transform in front of him? Can you picture the huge grin that spread across his face for the first time in years? Can you envision the blurred vision he experienced as tears of amazement and joy welled up in his eyes? All this just because Jesus felt compassion and cared enough to do something about it. He left that day rejoicing. His only worry must have been how to get rid of his old leper clothes and where to get a new wardrobe. He must have left Jesus shouting and jumping in the air with excitement. That day he went from being a leper to a leaper!

As we look at Jesus' life, we notice that He loved to touch people. His physical touch communicated so much. Ask the group, **What do you think Jesus' touch said to people?** It said, "I care. I'm here. It's going to be all right. Have hope. Don't give up. Don't worry. You matter to me. I accept you. I understand. I love you."

Jesus then told the man not to tell anyone about this incident. **Why do you think He said this?** One reason could have been that Jesus didn't want a mob around Him merely asking for physical healing. Another reason could have been that this early in His ministry, Jesus wanted the freedom to move from town to town preaching the Gospel. Huge crowds might have prevented Him from doing this. In reality, this is what happened (vs. 45). How ironic that Jesus told this former leper to be quiet and yet he told everybody. Jesus asks us to tell everybody, and yet we often keep silent!

Keep in mind that without God's grace, we could be just as sinful as anyone else, right? Not to mention the fact that most people expect Christians to condemn and judge. It takes them by surprise when we care instead. We need tender, compassionate hearts, hearts that can hurt and feel the pain others feel. Ask, **What is there in your life that could help you identify with what they are going through? Have you ever had a similar experience? If not, can you try and put yourself in their place and imagine what they must be going through?**

Pass out copies of "How Do You Feel?"(Resource 3A). **After rating your feelings in these situations, what did you learn about yourself?**

Link 3

Now Who's Touching Who?

Take a few minutes for a brainstorming session with your group. See how many different people they can name who have been know as being compassionate. Tell them that there are not limited to just people they know; those named can be a celebrity, a group of people or even an organization. Responses could include: doctors, nurses, disaster relief organizations (Red Cross, FEMA, Salvation Army, local rescue missions, etc.), the late Mother Teresa, their pastor, individuals who work with those who are mentally or physically handicapped, retirement home employees, etc.

Ask, **Why would you consider this person or group to be compassionate?** Because of the nature of what they do. **Do you think it is possible to work in an organization like this and still not have compassion?** Sure it is. Some people do it just as a job. But most genuinely care about people.

LEARNER LINK

Of course you want your group members to understand everything you're discussing. So periodically ask them, "Does that make sense?" or "What questions do you have about this?" This will not only encourage openness but also help them to see what you are trying to get across in the study. Repeating yourself is not a crime. Sometimes re-stating your point in different words is what helps the truth sink in. Or better yet, ask one or more of your students to put in their own words the truth you've just discussed. You can do this several times throughout the lesson if you like.

What challenges do you think these people face on a daily basis? What rewards do you suppose they get from their work? Some may include seeing others feel loved and cared for, knowing they are making a difference in other's lives, helping them out of trouble, and giving them a better life and standard of living.

How can you live out compassion as Jesus did? Invite various students to share here.

Sometimes moving from apathy to compassion is a matter of really seeing the needs around you. Jesus was moved with compassion after being confronted with their needs.

MAKING IT REAL

A big part of discipleship is encouraging your students to put what they have learned into action. As their leader, you should be constantly looking for teachable moments—times when you are together with the students, outside of your group time, in which you can encourage them to practice what they have been learning. Another great way to do this is to set up service projects or experiential learning times. Session five in this book provides what you need to set up one of these learning experiences.

Have a student read "Opportunity Knocks...Be Home" (Resource 3B). Use this as a more tangible way to help group members see themselves as models of compassion.

Invite your students to share some of the specific needs that they felt Jennifer, the girl with cerebral palsy might have. The options were:

Physical Needs

Spiritual Needs

Emotional Needs

Intellectual Needs

Friendship Needs

Invite your students to share what they wrote in answer to the question, What are some ways you could meet Jennifer's needs in a manner that says, "I really care about you'?

Hand out the student journal "Heart Check: A Practical Approach to Having Compassion for Others" and encourage your students to apply what they've learned in the next week as they study Scripture and apply it to their lives.

How Do You Feel?

Looking at the areas below, imagine them as real life situations. Rate each one on a scale of 1-7 concerning how much compassion you feel. Use the scale at the bottom of the page as your guide.

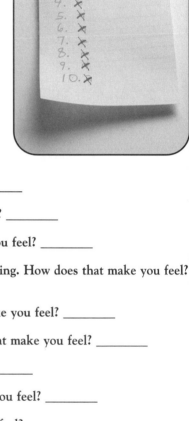

• People in a far away country are homeless because of a great earthquake. How does that make you feel? _____

• A little girl in your town is missing. How does that make you feel? _____

• You see a report about A.I.D.S. patients on the news. How does that make you feel? _____

• A family has a car wreck. Three members of a five-member family are killed. How does that make you feel? _____

• Your aunt is dying of cancer. How does that make you feel? _____

• A girl at your school gets pregnant. How does that make you feel? _____

• You find out a close friend is using drugs. How does that make you feel? _____

• A house in your neighborhood burns and the family loses everything. How does that make you feel? _____

• Someone you know has been sexually abused. How does that make you feel? _____

• The "bad guy" in your class gets arrested for drugs. How does that make you feel? _____

• A friend's dad just lost his job. How does that make you feel? _____

• You see a paralyzed person at a restaurant. How does that make you feel? _____

• Your little sister flunks a big math test. How does that make you feel? _____

• Your best friend gets "dumped" by his or her girlfriend or boyfriend. How does that make you feel? _____

• Someone in your youth group can't afford to go to the retreat. How does that make you feel? _____

> 1 – They deserve what they're experiencing
> 2 – I have no feeling either way
> 3 – That's too bad, but that's life
> 4 – I feel sorry for this person
> 5 – That makes me hurt inside for them
> 6 – I would like to help, but really there isn't much I could do
> 7 – I have to (and will) do something to help

Opportunity Knocks . . . Be Home

Jennifer is not your typical youth group member. Yes, she was raised in the church and has been coming every time the doors have been opened. She comes from a nice home and goes to the same school as everyone else. She is a regular girl in every way…. except one. Jennifer has cerebral palsy. As a condition normally caused by lack of oxygen to the brain in birth, it prevents certain parts of the brain from functioning properly, particularly physical motor skills like speech, walking and using the hands and feet. As a result, Jennifer walks with a noticeable limp, and though her intelligence is above average, she has difficulty communicating because of her speech.

Growing up, no one wanted Jennifer to be on his or her team. All her life, she has been made fun of by other kids. She has missed out on a lot of "normal" teenage activities and experiences—dating, sports, playing a musical instrument, going on class trips, driving, hiking, etc. In spite of this, Jennifer doesn't feel sorry for herself nor does she want anyone else to pity her. She accepts the reality of her condition, but still wants to be as normal as possible. Bottom line—she's 16 and in your youth group. So what do you do?

© PhotoDisc, Inc.

What specific needs to you think Jennifer might have? List them by category.

• Physical Needs

• Spiritual Needs

• Emotional Needs

• Intellectual Needs

• Friendship Needs

What are some ways could you meet Jennifer's needs in a manner that says, "I really care about you"?

HEART CHECK:
A Practical Approach to Having Compassion for Others

God desires that we go far beyond just knowing about the things we've discussed in this lesson. He wants us to allow our knowledge to be practical, to let it sink into and grow out of our lives. This section will help us think further about showing compassion to others.

LOOK IT UP

Below you'll find seven Scripture references, one for each day of the week. Each passage listed below has something interesting to say about relating to others' needs. Spend a few minutes each day looking up the passage and writing down a few (relevant) ideas that pop into your head.

DAY ONE: Psalm 103:1-14 (How many ways can you find that show God pours out His compassion on you?)

_____
_____
_____
_____

DAY TWO: Psalm 111:4-5 (God demonstrates His compassion on us by remembering His "covenant," or promise. What are some of God's promises to you?)

_____
_____
_____
_____

DAY THREE: Colossians 3:12-14 (What does "clothing yourself with compassion" practically look like, according to vss. 13-14? How did Jesus do this?)

_____
_____
_____
_____

DAY FOUR: Acts 3:1-10 (Where do you see compassion at work in this passage?)

_____
_____
_____

☺ TALK IT UP

Having compassion on others is not an overnight thing. It requires having our thinking process transformed (Romans 12:2). Knowing this is a matter of growth. Begin praying to the Lord throughout the day that He might cause you to see people the way He sees them. Ask Him to give you a heart of compassion and eyes of mercy. One way you can do this in prayer is to think of your own sin and how God has treated you with compassion. In addition, be totally honest and talk to your Heavenly Father about the people you struggle to have compassion for.

_____
_____
_____
_____
_____
_____
_____
_____
_____
_____
_____
_____
_____
_____
_____
_____
_____
_____
_____
_____
_____

DAY FIVE: Luke 15:11-20 (Why do you suppose there was such a compassionate response in this situation? Explain what you mean. What point was Jesus trying to get across with this story?)

_____

_____

_____

DAY SIX: 2 Samuel 9:1-13 (What do you see in the life of David that you would like to imitate?)

_____

_____

_____

DAY SEVEN: John 9: 1-12 (How did Jesus show compassion to this blind man? What else came out of this encounter?)

_____

_____

_____

_____

DO IT UP

If you're serious about caring about the world as Jesus did, you'll need an action plan. Here is one to follow:

STEP ONE: **Plan!**

Consider memorizing some Scripture concerning compassion. Pick one of the verses in the Heart Check section to begin with. Write down the verse(s) on a card to carry with you. But just memorizing isn't enough. You have to live it out. How will you do that this week? What are a few steps you might take?

STEP TWO: **Act!**

After a couple of days of putting your plan into action, how do you feel about it? Have you been consistent in following through? If you didn't and failed in some way, how did God respond to you? How will you take steps to become stronger?

STEP THREE: **Review!**

After all this study, do you think you could lead someone else in it? Maybe not officially teaching them, but could you guide them in a discussion? Would you be willing to voluntarily share with someone else what God has taught you about what compassion looks like? Who will that be? When will you do it?

LITTLE BIBLE BACKGROUND

Link 2

Leprosy was and is a horrible disease. The word is related to that of "scale," referring to the condition of the skin. Because there was no cure in Jesus' time, lepers were cast outside the city and forced to live in leper colonies. There was a phobia about leprosy, and it was believed you could get it if you touched someone who had the disease. It was illegal to greet a leper in public. There were laws made about how far away you were supposed to stand back from a leper, depending on which way the wind was blowing. Lepers emitted an awful stench. They were required to wear a bell around their necks and had to ring the bell when entering the city, shouting "Unclean, unclean!" (Lev. 13:45-46). They were outcasts who had no rights, no privileges and no hope. It was into this society and situation that Jesus Christ came. And He came not only to change society, but lepers too.

Link 3

Thinking about the examples you listed in Link 3 (Now Who's Touching Who). **What do you suppose are some of the keys to seeing others with the eyes of compassion? If we could peek into the spiritual world, we would see spiritual lepers walking around. And yet, instead of running from them, God desires us to run to them.** Ask students, **If we thought about sin as if it were physical leprosy, how do you suppose that might change the way we live? But as it relates to others, how would we react differently?** It would cause us to help others avoid sin and to have more compassion for those who fall into it.

ADVANCED LEARNERS

Link 2

Read Mark 6:30-34. **What was Jesus trying to do in vs. 31? What "spoiled" His plans (vss. 32-33)?** The crowds saw where He was going and ran ahead to the other side of the lake to meet Him. **How would you have responded in this situation? How did Jesus respond (vs. 34)?** He had compassion for them. **Why?** Because they were like sheep without a shepherd. **So what did Jesus do?** He taught them (vs. 34), and then He fed them (vss. 35-44). In a totally separate incident in Matthew 15:30-31, Jesus responded compassionately again. But this time, He not only fed people, but also healed all those who were sick, lame, blind, mute, and crippled. That's what it meant for Jesus to have compassion. He always felt something first, and then He did something.

Link 3

Why do you supposed so few people really care about others? From what might this selfishness stem? Read or review the story of the "Good Samaritan" found in Luke 10:25-37. **Who in this story do you expect to help the man?** Probably the priest, since he was supposed to be God's representative. **Why do you suppose he didn't stop to help?** Maybe he just didn't care. Maybe he was busy. Perhaps he didn't want to get dirty or bloody. He might have thought it was a trap. He could have thought the man was dead and didn't want to become "ceremonially unclean." He may have thought he was "above" that kind of ministry. Notice that all three of them "saw" the beaten man (vss. 31-33), but only the third man actually "felt" anything for him. **What did he feel?** Compassion. And his compassion caused him to go beyond just "feeling" something. It caused him to "do" something. **What did he do?** He bandaged his wounds, treated them, carried him to a local inn, and took care of him all through the night (vs. 34). **What point was Jesus making in this parable?** He was saying that when we show mercy and kindness, we prove ourselves to be a true neighbor. That's interesting, because the question the young man asked Jesus was "Who is my neighbor?" (vs. 29), but Jesus answered him by showing him how he could be a neighbor to those around him. **How will you train your eyes to see what Jesus saw?**

MOSTLY GUYS

Link 1

Needed (optional) old radio or alarm clock

Ask your guys if they have ever taken apart anything to see what was inside (like an engine, a watch, or a radio, etc.). Consider bringing an old radio or alarm clock to demonstrate. Say, **You can really understand something** when you take it apart. That way you get to see what makes it tick, what makes it function they way it does. Tell them that the way we get "inside" the heart of God, to see what He is really like is by looking at the life of Christ. Through Jesus, we can get into the heart of God by looking at how He showed compassion to others.

Link 3

Has anyone ever shown compassion to you? Were you ever spared punishment by your parents when you really deserved it? Ever had a flat tire and someone stopped and helped? Or better, when have you shown compassion to someone? Are you stronger in judgment or in compassion? Compassion isn't real until we apply it to real life situations. **To whom have you shown compassion before?**

MOSTLY GIRLS

Link 1

Draw your girls' attention to the school and church shootings that have taken place in the past few years. Download and print an article off the Internet if you can related to these situations. Ask students to share what they know about these incidents and give each girl an opportunity to contribute. Ask, **How did you feel when you heard the news? What was your first response? Have you ever wondered if that could happen in your school or church? If you could do anything for those who are still suffering, what would it be? How do you think God feels about those incidents? Does He care? How has He shown that He cares?**

Link 2

Sometimes reaching out in compassion can be both a challenge and a risk. Ask the group to brainstorm and share what they think Jesus might have been risking in touching this leper. They might respond by saying He may have risked being misunderstood by some people; He may have been ridiculed; He might have been considered unclean after touching the man; He might have lost His credibility among the religious elite, etc. **What do you risk when you show compassion to someone in need?** Keep in mind that sometimes showing compassion can be a popular thing (like helping out a family around Christmas time) and other times it can be very unpopular (like being friends with someone who is disliked at school). But either way, there are risks. **What are some of them?**

MEDIA

Link 1

Needed: CD, CD player

Play the song "Never Been Unloved" by Michael W. Smith (on the *Live the Life* CD). But first you might choose to read the words out loud. Ask your group to listen for all the ways in the song we come up short of God's standard. But then ask, **How does God respond to our failure? What never changes about Him?**

Link 2

Needed: Video, VCR

Rent the movie "The Man Without a Face," starring Mel Gibson. Use a short clip (most any that shows Mel Gibson will do) to demonstrate how awkward and difficult it is to live in a world where you are not "normal." Discuss how the man dealt with his disfigurement. Relate to the group how, in the remainder of the movie, a young boy develops a friendship with the man and how their relationship changes both of them. (Another movie option might be "The Elephant Man" starring Anthony Hopkins.)

EXTRA ADRENALINE

Link 2

Play a game where you divide students into partners. When you call out the names of two body parts, their job is to touch the two parts together. They have to hold that position until you call out another combination. Begin easy and work up to the difficult stuff. For example: Hand to hand. Shoulder to foot. Ear to elbow. Nose to knee. Head to foot. Chin to back, etc. After having some fun with this for a few minutes, transition by explaining that although Jesus most likely never played silly games like this, Jesus believed very strongly in making physical contact with others. He came to touch us, both physically as well as spiritually. And His touch was visible and tangible (it was always seen and felt). It always said, "I care." **How can you use physical touch to show kindness and concern?**

Link 3

If possible, go outdoors and play a game of old fashioned "freeze tag" with your group. One person is "it" and their job is to tag as many people as they can. When the person is tagged, they are "frozen" until another student can run by and "unfreeze" them by touching them. The goal of the person who is "it" is to try and freeze the entire group. But if this doesn't happen, rotate people into that role. Or another idea would be to play touch football for a bit before or after your lesson.

Point out that just like the whole purpose of the game was to touch other people, so Jesus' whole purpose in coming to earth was to touch us. He did this physically to show us how much He cared for us spiritually.

JUNIOR HIGH

Link 2

Ask your group members to imagine themselves as Jesus' disciples who witnessed this incredible scene with the leper. Tell them to picture "thought bubbles" over their heads (like in comic strips). As they listen and watch Jesus, what thoughts are popping into their minds? Ask them to interrupt you as you read the story to share what they imagine the disciples were thinking. Accept all reasonable comments. Encourage them to be very honest.

Link 3

Showing compassion is hard for the average junior high student. So to help here, be sure to make personal application to group members in this section. For example, you might say, "Chris, imagine that this leper was you. How would you feel?" Or you might put it this way: "Angela, what if you had a physical deformity (like Jennifer in Resource 3B). How would you like people to act towards you?"

Planning Checklist

LINK 1: The Heartbeat of God
❏ Mostly Guys
❏ Mostly Girls
❏ Media

LINK 2: Jesus Meets the Untouchable
❏ Little Bible Background
❏ Advanced Learners
❏ Mostly Girls
❏ Media
❏ Extra Adrenaline
❏ Junior High

LINK 3: Now Who's Touching Who?
❏ Little Bible Background
❏ Advanced Learners
❏ Mostly Guys
❏ Extra Adrenaline
❏ Junior High

THE EMBRACE OF LOVE

Key Questions

- How would you explain what the phrase Jesus "died in my place" means?
- What can I do to show my appreciation for what took place when Jesus died on the cross?
- How can I embrace the world with the love of Jesus?

Bible Base

John 3:16
Romans 5:8; 6:23
2 Corinthians 5:21
Ephesians 2:8-9

Supplies

- Pencils
- Bibles
- Copies of Resources 4A, 4B, Journal
- Poster Board
- Scissors
- Markers

Opener (Optional)

A Familiar Problem

If your students have been in church for any amount of time, they have heard that "Jesus died for their sins." However, the impact of this great truth may have faded for them over the years. This may especially be true of "churched" students, since they have likely seen the cross portrayed in everything from coloring books, cartoons, videos, Sunday school lessons, to sermons. As a result, their ears may have become dull to the message of God's love. When that happens, it's hard to properly respond in love back to Him. Use this time to help the group see how easy it is to "tune out" things we've heard over and over again. Ask them to raise their hands if they have ever heard an adult say the following things:

—Your room's a mess. It looks like a tornado hit it;—Be careful, or you'll poke your eye out;—I don't care what everybody else does. If everyone else jumped off a bridge, would you?;—Don't put your feet on the furniture;—Because I said so, that's why!;—Are you listening to me?;—Attention, students . . . ;—Call me when you get there;—Five more minutes on the phone, that's it!;—Be nice to your sister/brother;—We're doing this as a family;—What? Do you think I'm made of money?;—We'll have to wait and see;—I love you.

Follow this up by saying: **Isn't it scary that all adults somehow know to say these things? The point, of course, is that because we have heard these things over and over again, we can nod our heads and say "yes, sir, yes ma'am" while checking out mentally, can't we?**

Explain that the exact same principle is true when it comes to hearing about Jesus' death on the cross. Though it's not intentional, we subconsciously grow cold to the simple truth of the Gospel. Over time, we learn to agree in church when Jesus' death is talked about without really experiencing God's love for us through it. We can even agree in our heart with God about His sacrifice for us and still not allow Him to change our lives with that truth. **This lesson's challenge is for you to listen to God speak about His Son's sacrifice like you're hearing it for the first time. Try and forget what you've heard time and time again and try to see the cross for what it really is—God's way of saying "I love you."**

Link 1

What's the Big Idea?

Begin by reviewing last week's "Heart Check: A Practical Approach to Having Compassion for Others."

LEARNER LINK

We all know that discipleship is not fully accomplished just during small group Bible study time. Your students need your influence outside of group time as well. Plan time as a group to just hang out and have fun together. Try and spend a little time periodically with each student one on one. Think of this time as an investment of your life that will pay off during your group study time. Your students will listen and participate much more knowing that you have cared enough to be with them outside the group.

Here are some answers to the question "Why are we studying this again?":

1. **Only the Gospel can save the lost.** Good people don't go to heaven; only those who have their sins dealt with through what Jesus did on the cross do. Without Christ and His cross, there is no hope for eternal life. That makes this topic worth discussing again and again.

2. **We can't share what we don't *know*.** If we are going to embrace the world like Christ did, we have to know exactly what the Gospel is. We have to be clear about the message.

MAKING IT R E A L

One of the benefits of leading a small discipleship group is the chance to reach out to some of the parents and families of the students. Make a point any chance you get to talk with them and to let them know what you have been doing in your group. Parents appreciate that, and it can help them encourage their students at home. Not all of them may be Christians, so be aware that they are looking for the characteristics of Jesus in your life.

3. **We can't share what we don't *have*.** As we study this lesson, you will be able to erase doubts about your own salvation. You can leave this lesson with the assurance that you have a personal relationship with God.

4. **Many people believe in a false gospel.** We are surrounded by people who are trying to get to heaven by some way other than Christ. **What are some of those ways?** Being good, going to church, being religious, etc. They may sincerely want to go to heaven, but really don't know for sure how they can.

5. **God's love shown in the Gospel is what motivates us to share.** We don't tell others about Christ just because we're "supposed to." We should do it because we want to. Being motivated by His love overflowing out of us is one of the best ways to share Christ. This lesson will motivate you to be a witness for Him. Have students work on "Cross Views" from Resource 4A to better clarify what Christ and the cross really mean

Link 2

You Know It by Heart

Turn in your Bibles to John 3:16. But before you study it, from memory say the verse out loud as a group. Bring several different Bible translations with you and pass out a different version to each student or group of students. Go around the group and read the various translations noting the differences between them. As a group, choose one that the group likes the best. Memorize that translation of the verse and have students recite it the next time you meet.

Next tell your students that you're going to "dissect" John 3:16 together as a group project. The goal is to find out as much as possible about what this verse is saying. The verse contains several different parts. Think of them like pieces to a puzzle. Each piece reveals a part of the picture, that when put together, forms a perfect portrait of God's great gift of salvation to us. Write the verse on poster board and cut it apart as you go through it so group members have a visual of it. Here are the pieces:

"For God..."

Who are we talking about here? God the Father, the Creator of the universe. The Gospel begins with God, not humans. He initiated contact with us when we were unable to come to Him (John 6:44). He is the same God back in the Garden of Eden who pursued Adam and Eve after they sinned.

"...so loved"

According to this verse, what motivated the Father? His love. **What does this tell you about the kind of God He is?** He is a God of love (1 John 4:8). We don't know why God is the way He is. He just is. And love is not just a part of who God is. It influences everything He does, as well as all His actions. He is a loving God. He cannot be any other way. It's His nature to love. It's natural for Him. He is the originator and "inventor" of love.

"...the world"

Who is "the world" here? This refers to people. Every kind of people, every race, nationality, and background. This includes the best and most moral person to the lowest and most evil one. God simply loves all humans, the crown of His creation, even though we are sinners (Romans 3:23). **But have you ever wondered *why* God loves you? What reasons does He have? Does He *have* to love us because He made us? Is it because of something good in us (Rom. 7:18)? Or because we are good-looking, athletic, or popular? Is it because we love Him back so well? If not, then why?** The obvious conclusion is that God is under no obligation to love a sinful world. He loves us simply because He chooses to (Rom. 9:15). It pleases Him to love you, and knowing this ought to cause a sense of wonder in our hearts.

"...that He gave His one and only Son"

God's love for us motivated Him to do something about our lost and sinful condition. **And what did He do?** He sent His Son. Remind your students that Jesus is not a son in the human sense of the word. Jesus is God and fully equal with the Father and the Spirit (John 1:1-3; 8:58). Being called the Son means He shares the same nature as the Father. Jesus is unique. There is no one like Him. And because the Father, Son, and Spirit work together perfectly, they agreed to come and save sinners. The Father's role would be to send (John 3:16). The Son's would be to suffer and die (Rom. 5:8), and the Spirit's role would be to search, find, and draw us to Christ (John 16:7-11).

Ask students to think of the person who means more to them than anyone. A person who is more important to them than any possession. Someone for whom they would give up anything. Now ask, **Can you imagine personally sentencing this person to die?** Of course they can't. **Take it a step further and imagine sentencing that person to die in the place of a convicted murderer. How insane, right? And yet, that's what God did when He sent His Son. Do you see the sacrifice the Father made when He sent Christ to die for us? Can you feel the sense of loss heaven must have felt?** That's part of what it means to say, "For God so loved the world *that He gave His one and only Son....*"

"...that whoever believes in Him"

What do you think it means to "believe" in something? Ask them to explain what the word means in the following statements:

It is very possible that one or more students in your group have never understood the Gospel in this way. As a result, he or she may have responded to an invitation or even said a prayer of salvation without actually placing personal faith in Christ. Use this group time as an opportunity to be sensitive to their understanding of these truths. Consider giving them an occasion to trust Christ for salvation at the close of your group time. If this isn't the best option, then follow up with students who appear to be confused or uncertain about their relationship with God.

I believe in myself.
I believe in getting a good education.
I believe in my country's system of government.
I believe the world is round.
I believe in Jesus.
So what's the difference? Is it possible for someone to say they "believe in Jesus" without actually *believing* in Him? Yes. There is a difference between acknowledging the existence of Jesus, saying you think He was a good teacher, and actually placing personal faith in Him for salvation. To believe means to put faith in. To trust in. To commit to. To acknowledge. As you look at Scripture, you'll find that believing in Christ is portrayed in different terms and pictures.

Receiving Him—John 1:12
Opening the door (of your life)—Revelation 3:20
Coming to Him—John 6:35
Calling on the name of the Lord—Romans 10:13
Having faith in Him—Ephesians 2:8-9

But these are all describing the same thing—believing in the Son of God.

"...shall not perish but have eternal life."
God's desire is to save us from the punishment we all deserve. He does not want us to experience the wrath that will come upon those who do not have Christ. The very next verse tells us:

"For God did not send His Son into the world to condemn the world, but to save the world through Him" (John 3:17).

MAKING IT R E A L

Don't give your students the impression that it's easy to follow Jesus' example! If you don't acknowledge the challenges, some of your group members may leave with unrealistic expectations. Prepare your students for these unfortunate possibilities by talking honestly about how people may respond to them and risks that are involved in being a disciple of Jesus Christ. Rather than discouraging your group members, you may find that your straightforward approach actually motivates many of them.

Point out that in Scripture, eternal life means more than just living forever. Every person, Christian or not, will live eternally somewhere (Rev. 14:10-11). But beyond just the length of our existence, eternal life has to do more with the quality of our existence. To have eternal life means to experience and enjoy the most satisfying relationship with God possible. It means, according to Jesus Himself, to really *know* God (John 17:3). What salvation restores to us relates to what Adam and Eve lost in the Garden— knowing God and enjoying His presence. And that enjoyment will last forever. What we gain by becoming His children is even more exciting than the thought of what we miss, which is hell.

Link 3

A Little Court Reporting

Read the story "Case Dismissed" from (Resource 4B). You may want to ask your students to close their eyes as you read it. Discuss what they learned from the story. **What did you learn about God the Father? About Satan? About your own sin? About Jesus? At what point in the story were you most afraid? Most worried? Most relieved? Most joyful?**

Explain that even though this was a fictional drama, it is based on biblical truth. God really is a just and holy Judge (Hab. 1:13; Job 34:10; Ps. 77:13). He must judge and punish sin because He is righteous. No person will ever get to heaven unless that person has been made holy in God's sight (Matt. 5:48).

Satan truly is our enemy and he actually appears before God to accuse us and condemn us (Job 1:6-11; Rev. 12:10). But Jesus is always there to defend as our eternal Attorney (1 John 2:1-2; Heb. 7:25). At the cross, Jesus absorbed the consequences for our sin. Upon your accepting salvation, it was applied to your account. Now God is no longer your Judge. He's your Father (Rom. 8:15-16). Jesus literally embraced the world as He hung on the cross. This was one thing only Jesus could do, and He did it because He loved us so much.

As we attempt to embrace the world, we can tell unbelivers in our world about what Jesus did for them on the cross. We can point them to Jesus when they feel they've lost their way. We can give them the embrace of hope as we share the Gospel with them.

Hand out copies of the student journal "Heart Check: A Practical Approach to Embracing the Cross" and encourage your students to read the Scriptures, answer the questions, and apply the concepts to their lives.

Cross Views

Throughout history people have formulated different opinions and theories about the death of Jesus. The church has even officially condemned some of these theories. Below are some examples of these. **Looking at them, can you agree with what any of them say? What about them causes you to disagree? Where do they fall short in accurately describing the cross?**

1. The cross was a human tragedy, on the level of a Shakespeare play. There was nothing divine about it. It is just a sad story.

2. Jesus on the cross is a good example to us all of love and sacrifice. He is a model for us to follow.

3. The cross represents the death of a martyr. He was a man who died for something He believed in.

4. On the cross, Jesus was punished by the devil. He paid a ransom to Satan to buy us back from sin.

5. The cross represents Jesus dying in our place for our sin. It stands throughout time as the supreme symbol of love.

The cross certainly was a tragedy, humanly speaking. But it was all a part of God's plan to redeem human beings (Acts 2:23). And yes, Jesus death was an example of sacrificial love that we can follow in giving our lives up for others. But that was only a small part of the purpose of the cross. Jesus may be a martyr to some, but then again, martyrs don't come back from the dead. And in no way did Jesus pay any sort of ransom to the devil. It is not Satan's demands that had to be met, but rather God's. God was the One who needed to be satisfied with Christ's sacrifice for sin (Rom. 3:25;1 John 2:2).

In reality, Jesus was our substitute. He suffered in our place (Rom. 5:8; 2 Cor. 5:21).

CASE DISMISSED

Imagine yourself in the following scenario:

You wake up one morning to find that you're not in your bed, but instead, you are sitting in a courtroom. Looking around, you see the place is packed with people. On the other side of the aisle is a man with an evil grin on his face staring right at you. Seated beside you is a kind and gentle man who looks familiar but who's name you can't remember. You shake your head, trying to recall how you got here.

Just then the doors open and in walks the judge. His long, dark robe and serious countenance gives you chills. He looks like he means business. He sits down, bangs his gavel, and says, "Let's begin." The prosecutor stands and says, "My name is Satan and I'm here today to prove that the defendant deserves to be punished and sentenced to hell." For what seems like days, he proceeds to list every bad thing you have ever done. All the lies. The times you disobeyed your parents. The lust. The cheating. The hate. The missed witnessing opportunities. The apathy. The bad habits. The lack of love. You poor commitment to doing the things of God. Your broken promises. He even shows a few pictures and video clips of some of your worst moments. He is very thorough and leaves nothing out. He rests his case and sits down.

You have never been so embarrassed in your entire life. Your face is red. You wish you could crawl under a chair and hide. You feel such guilt and shame. You know that everything Satan has said is true. You begin to shudder with fear at what the judge may say and do next.

Then your lawyer stands to address the judge. "Your honor, I am forced to agree with the prosecuting attorney. The charges against my client are all true. There is no denying them. He/she is guilty as charged and deserves to be sentenced to hell." At this point you know that there is no hope for you. Your eyes begin to well up with tears.

"But," your attorney continues as he turns to look you in the eyes, "I have already received the awful consequence for his/her sin." It is only then that you realize your lawyer is Jesus Himself. With a smile of reassurance He continues. "I took for my client all the wrath of this courtroom. I gave my life for all his/her sins—past, present, and future. If you will check the Book of Life, you'll see his/her name is recorded there. He/she is banking on the work I've done."

Your eyes fill with tears again, but this time for another reason. You realize in a fresh way what Jesus has done for you. You can't believe how great His love is.

"Your Honor, I rest my case," Jesus says, and sits down beside you with His strong hand on your shoulder. The Judge slams down his huge gavel with a sense of finality. "This person is free to go. The penalty has already been paid in full. Case dismissed!" The courtroom explodes with applause and you stand and embrace your Savior. You never want to let go of Him as you hear Him whisper in your ear, "I love you." As you turn to leave, you ask Him "Lord, have you ever lost a case?" Smiling, Jesus responds, "Everyone who has ever come and asked me to represent them in this court has received the same verdict . . . . not guilty."

HEART CHECK:
A Practical Approach to Embracing the Cross

God desires that we go far beyond just knowing about the things we've discussed in this lesson. He wants us to allow our knowledge to be practical, let it sink in, and have results from this knowledge grow out of our lives. This section will help us think further about understanding and appreciating Christ's sacrifice.

LOOK IT UP

Below you'll find seven Scripture references, one for each day of the week. Each passage listed below has something interesting to say about how Jesus Christ embraced the world in love. Spend a few minutes each day looking up the passage and writing down a few (relevant) ideas that pop into your head.

DAY ONE: Ephesians 1:1-14 (How many blessings of salvation can you find in this passage?)

_____

_____

_____

DAY TWO: Romans 8:1-4 (What did Jesus' death do for you that the Old Testament law could never do?)

_____

_____

_____

DAY THREE: Galatians 5:16-22 (What is the struggle all Christians have even after salvation, and how does Jesus enable us to overcome it?)

_____

_____

_____

_____

DAY FOUR: Luke 9:57-61 (What did these people say in response to their challenge to follow Jesus? How did the Lord respond to them?)

_____

_____

_____

☺ TALK IT UP

This prayer time may be the most meaningful and personal of all for you. Consider going for a "prayer walk" somewhere you can be alone and talk out loud to the Lord. Just spend this time telling Him how much you are grateful for what He has done for you. See if you can spend this prayer time without actually *asking* for anything, but rather just thanking and praising Him.

DAY FIVE: Colossians 2:6-7 (How does God desire that we grow in our new relationship with Him?)

_____
_____
_____
_____

DAY SIX: Matthew 27:27-50 (Where can you find Jesus' love for you in this passage? List as many ways as you can.)

_____
_____
_____
_____

DAY SEVEN: Luke 19:10 (What were Jesus' two main reasons for coming to earth? How did He accomplish those two things in your life?)

_____
_____
_____

DO IT UP

If you're serious about showing love and compassion as Jesus did, you'll need an action plan. Here is one to follow:

STEP ONE: **Plan!**

What are some tangible ways you can show Jesus' love as you embrace the world? Be specific here. Write these ways down and carry them with you all week, taking them out from time to time to remind you. Or consider carrying a note card in your pocket with the names of people you know who need Jesus that you could embrace.

STEP TWO: **Act!**

Set your alarm to get up a few minutes early this week just to spend time with the Lord. If mornings aren't your thing, how about on your lunch hour or after school? What difference did it make to carry the note card with unbelivers' names on it?

STEP THREE: **Review!**

After completing this spiritual exercise, think about what you need to embrace people with Jesus' love. How will you guard yourself against apathy and indifference to the many people you meet?

LITTLE BIBLE BACKGROUND

Link 1

God wants us to be ready to tell anyone about our faith at any time (1 Pet. 3:16). One way to do this more effectively is to know Scripture better. What might be some other ways? Challenge students to read through the Bible in a year to give them an overview of Scripture. Specifically, your students need to also prepare themselves to answer objections related to sharing their faith. You may want get a copy of *Don't Check Your Brains at the Door* by Josh McDowell. It explains in brief and understandable language how a teenager can effectively defend his/her faith.

Link 2

Share this before talking about John 3:16. A crucifixion was a horrible thing. It was a very slow and painful death. Stretched on a beam, the condemned criminal was nailed through the wrists and ankles with long metal spikes. Prior to the crucifixion, there were severe floggings. Often the criminal would die from the beatings before ever making it to the cross. But because of the placement of the nails, the person could hardly lift himself up to draw air into the lungs. Thus, most died from suffocation. If this had not occurred within a prescribed period of time, the legs were broken across the shins to prevent the person from lifting himself up to breathe. Bodies would hang on crosses for days, and many times be eaten by vultures or wild animals.

ADVANCED LEARNERS

Link 2

How can a person be sure he or she is a Christian? This is a relevant question because most Christians at one time or another have some doubts. Explain that there are many reasons why individuals might doubt their salvation, such as ongoing struggles with sin and temptations, slower than expected spiritual growth, a childhood faith decision that they didn't understand, an emotional conversion experience, an *un*emotional conversion, a period of time between salvation and actual growth, or doubt placed there by Satan. Reinforce the truth that the issue in salvation is trusting Christ. Every person who has ever come to Christ and placed faith in Him can have assurance of salvation as a child of God (John 6:37).

Link 3

Take a walk through Acts 17 and notice how the Apostle Paul shared the Good News with his world. **How did he embrace his world as Jesus did? What did he see?** (vs. 17) He saw the idols in Athens and that motivated him to share Christ with the people there. He was an observer of his culture. **How did he speak to them? What did he do next?** (17) He began reasoning with them on their level, about their world. He knew what they believed and thought. He found a point of contact. **Did Paul get mad when he wasn't received at first?** (vss. 18-21) No, he had patience with them. **What questions was he able to answer for them?** (vss. 22-31) He told them all about the God they didn't know and what He was like. He showed how God could meet their deepest needs. **Finally, did he force them to make a decision?** (vss. 32-34) Yes and no. By telling them about God, he was bringing them to a fork in the road. But the final decision was theirs. He didn't give up on them.

MOSTLY GUYS

Link 1

Invite your guys to share about a time they made a sacrifice for someone else. Such as letting someone else play in a sporting event instead of them, giving up their seat on a crowed bus, etc. Then ask your guys to share about a time when someone made a sacrifice for them. Explain that God's sacrifice of His Son is something we can never fully understand, but we can fully appreciate.

Link 2

Have each of your guys go through John 3:16 again. This time, however, have them substitute their name for the phrase "the world." Ask them if they ever feel like the Bible is impersonal and vague at times, and if so why? Explore with them ways they can read and apply Scriptures in a more personal way. **How can we look at the Bible as God's personal love letter to us? What practical steps would you take in your Bible study time? What would you need to change? What reading or study habits would you need to break?**

MOSTLY GIRLS

Link 1
At times, it's good to ask the really hard questions. Give your girls a chance to do a little self-evaluation with the following questions: **Does Christ seem real to you, or is He feel like a character in a book? Do you feel like you know Him in a personal way? Do you know what that means? Do you believe your lifestyle is able to convince people of the reality of Christ in you? Would your family say that your Christianity is real and genuine? What decisions do you need to make in order to grow in these areas?** Ask if any of the girls want to share how they would answer any of the above questions. Consider sharing out of your own life how these questions have affected you.

Link 2
Ahead of time, get some poster board and cut it into as many equal size pieces as the number of group members. Leave them blank for now, but when your group gets there, give each one a marker and ask them to write John 3:16 on one side of the card using the translation the group chooses. Then assign them each a portion of the verse. (Depending on the group size, some members may have the same section of the verse, but that's O.K.) Allow each group member to tell what their particular phrase means to them. Have them take the cards home to put up on their bulletin board, mirror, or somewhere else that can serve as a reminder to them of what Christ did for them on the cross.

MEDIA

Link 1
Needed: Two or three video cameras
First, get two or three video cameras, then go to a nearby shopping center. Organize the group into teams and send them out to get people's answers to the following questions. Make sure your students pick a variety of people to interview. (Encourage them to ask people first if they can interview them and also share with the people that this is a short project for their youth group). The questions are: **What do you think of when you see a cross? What does the cross mean to you? What does it symbolize?** Go to one of the student's houses and watch the video clips together. Beyond the inevitable laughter, discuss people's responses to your questions and talk about how what they says reflects today's culture. **Were the answers they got "religious" ones? What was the most surprising response they received?**

Link 3
Needed: CD, CD player (or hymnals) guitar (optional)
Get copies of a few songs about the cross or Jesus' death that the whole group is familiar with. You may even want to check out a few classic hymns such as "The Old Rugged Cross." Close your group time by singing a few of the songs in responsive worship. See if one of your students can play a guitar and help lead the singing. Use one of the songs as a guide during your group prayer time. Pray that the truth of these songs about the cross will penetrate your students' hearts.

EXTRA ADRENALINE

Link 2
A slightly different activity from the one in the media section would be to pack the group into your car and drive around town seeing how many crosses you can find in 30 minutes. Check out the mall, churches, stores, cemeteries, etc. Give a prize to the ones who find the most. Or consider standing in front of the mall and surveying people wearing crosses. A few volunteers could ask these people why they wear the cross and what it means to them. Other students could write down the people's responses. Talk about the different answers over ice cream or a snack.

Link 3

Call your students ahead of time and ask them to bring one personal possession that means a lot to them. It has to be something very valuable (though not necessarily expensive). During the group time, have them tell about their possession and why it is important to them (where they got it, when, and from whom, etc.). Then ask them what it would take to persuade them to give up that possession. Do this for each student. Transition by allowing them to discuss what it must have meant for God the Father to give up God His Son for us.

JUNIOR HIGH

Link 1

Needed: saltshaker

Bring a saltshaker with you and set it in the middle of the group. Ask your students to try and list as many uses for salt as they can. Then ask, **What does eating too much salt do to us?** Obviously it makes us thirsty. Jesus said "We are the salt of the earth" (Matthew 5:13). **How would you go about creating a thirst in someone else's life for what you have in Christ?** Brainstorm with your group about this. Then have students read John 4:1-15. See how many ways you can observe how Jesus built bridges to this woman. **How did He help create a thirst for God in her? What was the result?**

Link 2

Give your students a blank sheet of paper and challenge them in the next 24 hours to write out their testimony. You can encourage them to use the following guidelines: First, talk about their life before they came to know Christ (if they became Christians at an early age, then ask them to say what the Bible says about them before they were converted). Second, how did they come to know Christ? Where were they? How old were they? Who was there? What led up to it? Why did they feel like they needed Christ? And third, how has Christ made a difference in their lives? Ask them to be prepared to share their testimony with you or the group the next time you get together. Or you might even consider a special time such as over dinner or during a large group time. Remind them that in order to embrace the world with Jesus' love, they need to know how to share with those who might not know Jesus.

Planning Checklist

LINK 1: What's the Big Idea?
- ❏ Little Bible Background
- ❏ Mostly Guys
- ❏ Mostly Girls
- ❏ Media
- ❏ Junior High

LINK 2: You Know It by Heart
- ❏ Little Bible Background
- ❏ Advanced Learners
- ❏ Mostly Guys
- ❏ Mostly Girls
- ❏ Extra Adrenaline
- ❏ Junior High

LINK 3: A Little Court Reporting
- ❏ Advanced Learners
- ❏ Media
- ❏ Extra Adrenaline

REALITY CHECK: PRACTICING YOUR EMBRACE

About This Session

This bonus session is designed to help your group members understand discipleship in a deeper, more hands-on way. The four sessions of this book cover how God has shared His great love for us and can share it through us. True discipleship involves the heart, the head, and the hands. During this session you'll give your students a chance to take the things that they are learning and experiencing and put them into practice in the real world. This experiential learning time is a good way to wrap up your four weeks of study, but it can also be done at any point throughout the study.

Check It Out

All through these sessions, you have been challenging your students to take the example of Christ and to live out the truths of each study. However, this session is designed to encourage the group as a whole and to put into practice the things they have learned. Some students may have more experience than others, so encourage the more mature ones to look after those who may be taking a "first step."

One option you might consider would be to brainstorm with the group concerning their natural circle of influence. Begin where your students already have a platform for ministry. Where are they already in a position to "embrace the world," not as a newcomer but as a friend? Could they volunteer to assist a student government organization or a particular club or team at school? Is there an upcoming project in one of these areas where the group's "power" might be useful? Could they help build something, raise funds, decorate, plan, or promote the activity or project? Remind your students that they can do any or all of these things, all the while, rubbing shoulders with people who need Christ, and establishing friendships with them . . . in their world . . . on their level . . . in their language.

If that is not an option, consider volunteering where one of your students works. It could be a day of free labor. By doing this, you could say as a group "We care. We want to help. We expect nothing in return."

Take It Deeper

If your students are inclined, take this idea a step further and spend more than just one afternoon or Saturday lending a hand. Consider making this a regular ministry activity (as the commitment of your group and the need allows). This will create an even greater sense of credibility with those you are trying to reach. Keep in mind that many times Jesus met a physical, tangible need before He brought salvation to those in need.

Along those lines, encourage your group to look for specific needs among those with whom they are working. As they work alongside others, they will no doubt talk to them. Challenge them to listen for family, financial, emotional, friendship, and spiritual needs. Ask students to look for that common ground on which to build a bridge to that person. Look for a way to identify and relate. Listen with compassionate ears. Encourage your students to accept these people where they are spiritually, but also be willing to share the Gospel with them at any opportunity.

Think It Through

You will definitely need a time where you can discuss what happened during your time serving out in the world. Plan a meal someplace when you can talk and be relaxed. Be aware that some of your student's experiences will be more "successful" than others. Be sensitive to this and be sure to celebrate most of all the willingness of your students to step out in faith, to be used by God. Consider using the following questions to stimulate your thinking as you review together:

• What were your thoughts as you stretched out of your comfortable boundaries to embrace people with Jesus' love?

• Were you ever hesitant to embrace a certain person? Why? Were you able to overcome your inhibitions?

• Did it seem more difficult or easier than you had imagined to get involved in people's lives and embrace them as Jesus did?

• How do you think people responded to you?

• Were you able to "get into their world" as you attempted to embrace them with Jesus' love?

• What difference do you suppose it made that you went to them and helped them with something as opposed to just inviting them to church? What did that communicate to them?

• What do you think Jesus might do through you in this person's life?

• What lessons did you learn from these lessons on embracing the world as Jesus did? What did Jesus do in your life as a result of your willingness to serve?

• How does it feel to embrace the world of people as Jesus did?

Make sure that you praise your students publicly, not just during the group time but in other places as well. Ask them what this study has meant to them and how has it has made a difference in their lives. Close your time in prayer, thanking God for allowing you to follow in Jesus' footsteps by embracing the world like Him. Specifically, thank God for the way you have learned and been able to put into practice Jesus' example of identifying, accepting, caring, and even "suffering" a little for the sake of other people. Praise Him that He is the kind of God who would do that for you.

Name	Address	Phone	Parent Names	e-mail	B-day	Notes
1.						
2.						
3.						
4.						
5.						
6.						
7.						
8.						
9.						
10.						
11.						
12.						
13.						
14.						
15.						

Lift IT UP

Ephesians 3:16 "I pray that out of his glorious riches he may strengthen you with power through his Spirit in your inner being, so that Christ may dwell in your hearts through faith. And I pray that you, being rooted and established in love, may have power, together with all the saints to grasp how wide and long and high and deep is the love of Christ, and to know this love that surpasses knowledge—that you may be filled to the measure of all the fullness of God."

Learn how you can teach your teens to build rock-solid relationships with Jesus and each other.

BRING 'EM BACK ALIVE is a unique, 12-book study series that shows the all-too-human side of major Bible figures—and how God used them greatly. Each book contains 5 sections . . . focusing on characters like Peter, David, Ruth, and many others.

NEW!

CUSTOM DISCIPLESHIP takes a step beyond asking "What Would Jesus Do?" This 16-title series equips kids with the answers—they'll find out exactly what Jesus did in all kinds of relevant everyday situations, covering topics like measuring success, loving God's Word, and handling opposition.

CUSTOM CURRICULUM effectively reaches teens with proven programs that encourage and challenge them. More than 30 titles let you choose from over 150 options that are great for small groups and large groups. They fit within short meeting times or long. And the materials work for seasoned Christian kids as well as the unchurched.

Choose from Junior High/Middle School titles or the High School series.

QUICK STUDIES inspire genuine self-discovery through Old & New Testament Bible studies. They're extremely relevant to the issues faced by teenagers, and they're interactive—using games, surveys, and case studies to make kids think and open up. More than 40 sessions, 10 titles in all.

To order now
Call 1-800-323-7543
In Canada, call 1-800-263-2664